INTRODUCTION TO
ELECTRONIC CHART NAVIGATION

With an Annotated ECDIS Chart No. 1

STARPATH

ISBN 978-0-914025-57-3

Published by

Starpath Publications

3050 NW 63rd Street, Seattle, WA 98107

Manufactured in the United States of America

www.starpathpublications.com

10   9   8   7   6   5   4   3   2   1

Contents

Nomenclature and Sources

Historically, documents called "Chart No. 1" have actually been *printed booklets* that include all the chart symbols, along with their explanations. At the time of inception of this convention, charts were indeed paper, and Chart No. 1 was in effect a folded up paper chart of symbols alone, no land or water, and hence, for effective chart use, it would be the first "chart" you would want to look at. Traditional forms of Chart No. 1 are available from most nations that produce and distribute charts from their respective hydrographic offices.

The International Hydrographic Organization (IHO) document called "ECDIS Chart No. 1" is an extension of that traditional paper chart concept into the age of electronic charts. ECDIS stands for electronic chart display and information system. The IHO edition of "ECDIS Chart No. 1" is actually a set of special electronic navigational charts (ENC) made up of just the chart symbols, and, as with standard ENCs, you find out what a symbol means by clicking it on the computer screen. This set of nine, 1:14,000 electronic charts, when installed into a charting program, is positioned in the desert of central Mali, near 15 N, 5 W.

This special set of ENCs is available from the IHO, primarily for navigation program developers, so they can confirm their rendering of the symbols on the screen. It seems not to have been intended for public use, and indeed it would not be particularly beneficial to mariners underway using ENC. If they want to know the meaning of a symbol on an ENC in front of them, they would just click it; they would not need a separate chart of symbols.

Nevertheless, there remains a valuable role for a comparison of the electronic chart symbols and their corresponding paper chart symbols. NOAA recognized this early on, and in May of 2013 published the 12th edition of *U.S. Chart No. 1*, which, for the first time, showed the ECDIS standard electronic chart symbols and the paper chart symbols side by side. *U.S. Chart No. 1* is in effect another "ECDIS Chart No. 1," returning to the historic (printed) sense of the title. *U.S. Chart No. 1* is available as a free PDF download, or in print from several commercial outlets.

Chapter 4 of this book is based on the ECDIS symbols section of *U.S. Chart No. 1*, which we have reformatted, annotated, and cross referenced to other sections of this book. This book is not, however, intended as a substitute for *U.S. Chart No. 1* on any level. We do not include paper chart symbols and we have abbreviated the ECDIS parts as well. We strongly recommend that not just every vessel, but indeed every mariner, have a copy of *U.S. Chart No. 1*. You can go to the NOAA web site and download the PDF to your phone!

The British Admiralty publication N5012, *Admiralty Guide to ENC Symbols used in ECDIS* (1st edition, June, 2012) is also in effect an "ECDIS Chart No. 1," but that name is not used. We have chosen to call our Chapter 4 "Annotated ECDIS Chart No. 1." In principle it could be called "Annotated ENC Chart No. 1," or "Annotated Electronic Chart No. 1," but the actual symbols discussed are those specified by the ECDIS standard, which is what all electronic chart programs use as a guide, so it seems fair to us to shake that name loose from its esoteric origins.

In addition to *U.S. Chart No. 1*, our other primary resources have been the IHO publications *S-57, IHO Transfer Standard for Digital Hydrographic Data*, and *S-52, Specifications for Chart Content and Display Aspects of ECDIS*. In essence, the purpose of this book is to translate into useful terms those parts of those resources that are most relevant for routine navigation using electronic charts.

IMPORTANT NOTE

Every effort has been made to confirm the veracity of the content of this book. This is, however, a broad subject, open to interpretation in some cases, and potential errors in all cases. The author and publisher cannot warrant it is free of errors or omissions.

The book includes symbols and explanations used on electronic navigational charts, but it does not provide an exhaustive representation of all scenarios that might be encountered.

The selection and choice of screen shots from various sources does not reflect a preference or promotion of any particular charting program manufacturer.

Acknowledgments

First and foremost I thank Tobias Burch for his collaboration on all phases of the book. Beside creating all of the graphics, he designed the text and cover, and provided invaluable editing on both text and graphics. This project literally would not have been possible without his participation. I am also pleased to thank Starpath instructor Larry Brandt for once again applying his sharp editor's eye, finding needed corrections and clarifications throughout.

The NOAA Office of Coast Survey invites queries and comments on their products, and we have benefited immensely from that service. Many individuals there helped us understand the nuances of electronic charts, which has improved several aspects of this book. We thank them again here and remain grateful for their assistance.

During our study of electronic charts we benefited from the use of several navigation programs, and we remain grateful to these companies for the support they offered during the process. These include in alphabetic order: Coastal Explorer (Rose Point Navigation), ENC Online (NOAA), Expedition (Expedition Marine), MacENC (GPSNavX), OpenCPN, PolarView (Polar Navy), SeeMyENC (SevenCs), and TZ Navigator (Nobeltec).

I am also pleased to thank Brian Voss, Librarian at the NOAA Regional Library in Seattle. He has many times shown us the irreplaceable value of a real library and real librarian in the age of the internet. Thanks again for all your help over the years.

Our goal with this publication is to help mariners make the transition from traditional navigation using paper charts and associated printed publications to the use of an electronic charting system (ECS) that relies on some digital form of nautical charts.

An ECS is a software program that incorporates GPS signals and other sensor data so as to display a vessel's moving position on a digital chart, along with crucial derived parameters such as course over ground (COG) and speed over ground (SOG), among others. In it's simplest form, it can be a handheld GPS with a rudimentary base map; in its most sophisticated form it can be a complex system that meets the highest international standards of safe, efficient ship navigation. The type of ECS in use plays a key role in how we read and interact with digital charts.

There are two broad categories of digital charts, both of which are widely used internationally. They are distinguished by the nature of the digital files that represent the charts. The two chart file types are *raster charts* and *vector charts*.

1.1 Raster Charts

A raster chart is a graphic image of a region of the earth. They are photographic images that have been georeferenced, meaning each pixel location on the image has associated with it the corresponding latitude and longitude of the point shown in the image.

A raster chart can be made from an image of a street map, topographic map, or satellite image. A cellphone app following your position across a satellite image is an ECS using raster charts. For the discussion at hand, the most important type of raster chart is one made from a photographic image of an official paper nautical chart. Electronic charts made from official paper charts are called *raster navigational charts* (RNC).

On the display screen of an ECS, an RNC looks just like the paper chart it was made from, except that in this digital format the image can be zoomed, panned, rotated, and digitally annotated to carry out traditional navigation plotting. Thus a key point in the use of RNCs is that the chart symbols, labels, and chart notes are identical to those of traditional paper charts, because they are indeed just georeferenced pictures of the paper charts.

When using only RNCs, the navigator's transition from using paper charts to using digital charts is wholly a matter of learning the use of the navigation software that displays the charts, which is generically referred to here as the ECS. For example, how do we download and install the electronic charts; input our GPS signals to follow our vessel across the chart; how to use electronic range and bearing tools; how to set up waypoints and routes; and how to monitor our progress along that route using the electronic tools in the software.

Another factor that remains the same when going from paper charts to RNCs is our dependence on related navigation publications, such as the *U.S. Coast Pilot* and *Light List*. These documents contain crucial navigation information that is not shown on paper charts, and consequently not included in the RNC.

Since digital versions of these crucial navigation publications are readily available, some ECS programs have incorporated access to this supplemental data from within the software. This is one of the virtues of using electronic navigation in the first place, regardless of the chart type in use.

For example, place names in the *U.S. Coast Pilot* often include the Lat-Lon of the location, so an ECS program can include *U.S. Coast Pilot* data in such a way that a user could search on a place name, or mouse-click a specific place on the chart, and *U.S. Coast Pilot* information for that region will show up on a supplemental screen. This type of functionality is an asset to that ECS product, but it is not related to the chart in use. This extra information has been included by the ECS software manufacturer; it is not part of the RNC itself. Likewise, many ECS programs include tide and current overlays that can be displayed on the chart. These are a great asset to navigation, both when planning and when underway.

Of the many types of raster charts we might use, it is good policy to reserve the name "RNC" to those made specifically from the official paper charts issued by a national hydrographic office. The International Hydrographic Organization (IHO) website lists the member nations. A geo-referenced satellite image, or other raster chart provided by third parties, would not be called an RNC.

1.2 Vector Charts

In contrast to the static images of a raster chart, a *vector chart* is a dynamic depiction of the charted area that is created by the ECS software program from a database of nautical chart data and then drawn on the ECS display. A vectorized depth contour, for example, is not a picture of the depth contour shown on the paper chart, it is a curved line that is drawn on the screen each time the user displays the chart region that includes it, or changes the zoom level. A curved contour on a vector chart is a series of connected straight-line segments from one point to the next along the contour. The contour is stored as a table of Lat-Lon positions along that depth. The size of the steps along the line is determined by the scale of the chart so the curve appears a smooth line at the working scales. Likewise, land boundaries, and other areas on the chart are created on the wing from database entries. Even the symbols themselves are drawn out individually each time they are needed.

Because the entire chart is just a database of text and numbers, vector charts are inherently smaller file sizes than the corresponding high resolution graphic images of a raster chart. As such, a mariner can have a tremendous number of vector charts at hand for any voyage on a single CD, thumb drive, or plug-in chip for their ECS. Likewise, portable GPS devices can include very large areas in high detail using vector charts.

Most of the console navigation units used on vessels rely on vector charts, often in a proprietary format unique to the manufacturer. The main virtue of the vector format, however, is not the file size, but their ability to include many layers of information about the charted objects and the ability of the ECS to let mariners customize the display to varying degrees. With an RNC you have the option to change the display color palette in some ECS programs to best meet ambient light conditions (daylight, dusk, night), but that is about it. With vector charts you can not only change the display palette, you can choose the depth contour patterns, show or hide labels, and even simplify the symbology used for the aids to navigation (ATON). More sophisticated programs have more sophisticated options.

More importantly, you can view very detailed information about every object shown on the chart with a mouse click (called *cursor pick*) that pops up a table listing the properties (attributes) of the object. These crucial data are often more in-depth than can be found on the corresponding paper chart.

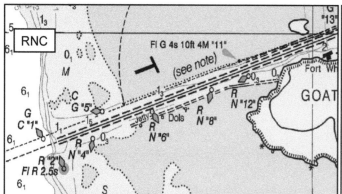

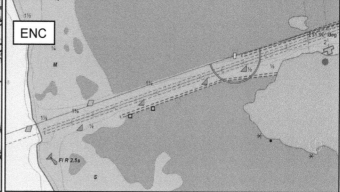

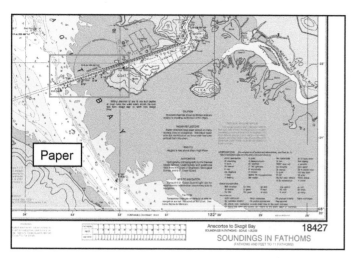

Figure 1.2-1. *A segment (red) of a paper chart (bottom left), shown as an RNC (top left), and ENC (top right). The RNC display is the same as the paper chart. The ENC is a vectorized presentation. Notable distinctions discussed later include customization of the ENC display regarding depth contours, labels, boundary and symbol styles, and more, along with the absence of terrain details on the ENC.*

But just as there are different types of raster charts, there are different types of vector charts as well. Many commercial companies create their own proprietary vector charts. These are all based on official government charts to some level, but it is only market competition that dictates how thorough, accurate, and up-to-date they are. In this book, however, we are only addressing official vector nautical charts produced by national hydrographic offices. Official vector charts all adhere to the same standard of content prescribed by the IHO called *S-57, IHO Transfer Standard for Digital Hydrographic Data.* Vector nautical charts produced to this standard are called *electronic navigational charts* (ENC). The name "ENC" applies only to S-57 adherent charts.

1.3 RNC versus ENC

In a sense, the use of RNCs is a traditional approach to electronic chart navigation, whereas ENCs are the future of electronic chart navigation. The many advantages of ENCs are not limited only to those already mentioned (more information and user customization). Since the software knows where you are, and it knows what is on the chart in front of your vessel icon, you can define anti-grounding zones in the direction of your COG (course over ground) to warn you of approaching hazards or shallow water. You can also highlight the visible arc of navigation lights in the vicinity to aid your visual navigation. There are numerous safety and efficiency features available to the navigator using an ENC.

Beyond that, because an ENC is a database, it is much easier and economical to update and distribute than the graphic or paper products are. An ENC can be updated in

seconds. The more mariners rely on this form of charting, the more efficient the process becomes, which is a benefit to both mariners and producers. With all the layers of information the ENC contains, the description of each ATON (aid to navigation) and geographic object on the chart improves over time.

An ENC, for example, will always tell us the height of a light above mean high water, just as an RNC would do. But, even if the latest ENC does not tell us that this particular light is on a 80-foot-tall, black-and-white-striped, cement tower, which itself is on a hill that is 45 feet above mean sea level, as the producing agency learns more about the object—with the help of mariners who know it well and take the trouble to report their observations—the information will eventually make it into the ENC. There is a limited amount of information that can be put onto a paper chart (RNC) within its own standards of production, whereas there are extensive attribute options for objects on an ENC. The United Kingdom Hydrographic Office (UKHO) already has a popular app for mobile devices, designed for mariners to make quick reports of charting discrepancies or additions they find underway. NOAA has a similar online service. Both respond promptly to all submissions.

As a further example, there are numerous lights or lighted buoys on RNCs whose labels do not include the nominal range that is crucial to predicting the visible range. In some cases, that is because it is not known. In other cases, however, this range is known and presented in the *Light List;* it is just not on the RNC. The latest edition of an official ENC, on the other hand, should include within it all *Light List* information that is known about that light, and thus we get this information directly from the ENC, when we could not get it from an RNC. For U.S. products, the

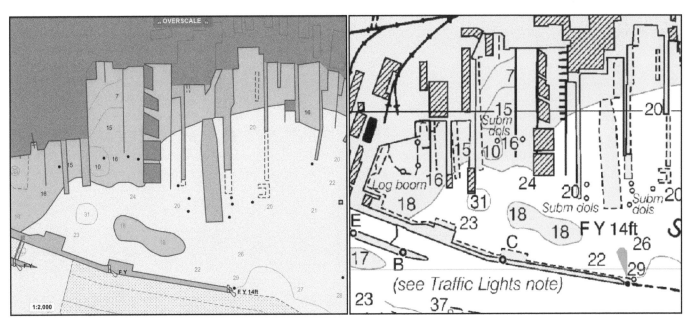

Figure 1.3-1. *ENC (left) and RNC (right) of the same docks area. Note breakwater lights shown on the ENC are relegated to a chart note in the RNC—an advantage of the ENC that also applies to some bridge lights.*

Light Lists and charts (ENC, RNC, and PDFs) are all updated weekly, so an updated ENC is equivalent to both an updated chart *and* an updated *Light List*.

Another advantage of ENCs is that in some cases there are no RNC counterparts at the scale we want. Carefully surveyed harbors can be nicely presented on a large scale ENC showing more detail or a cleaner display than possible with the available RNC. See Figure 1.3-1. In other cases, zooming in on an ENC can offer clearer navigation than possible on an RNC, although we must always be alert when using a chart that is "over-zoomed" (Section 2.3). The clean vector display may imply a chart precision that is not justified.

On the other hand, mariners accustomed to RNCs may find the conspicuous absence of land elevation contours on ENCs limiting to common piloting practice. These contours are part of the S-57 standard, but ENCs do not yet include them in the database. Other aspects of the terrestrial presentation are also significantly abbreviated on existing ENCs, but we anticipate this will improve. This subject is discussed further in Section 2.10.

ENCs are the charts of the future, and indeed they are the types of charts in use daily by thousands of professional mariners around the world. But, for the many other professional and non-professional mariners who are just beginning to use electronic charts, there is much to be learned. Moving into ENC navigation, we must not only learn the new symbology—which is actually not that different from what we are used to—but also confront new conventions and classifications of charted objects. Not to mention that some of the *virtues* of ENCs, such as customization of the display, can be disconcerting at times. We are accustomed to charts looking the same every time we use them. With the option to change the color pattern of waters between depth contours, and the style and labeling of the symbols themselves, a particular charted region can be made to look rather different.

With this in mind, it is a good idea to treat the ENC chart display much as we would treat radar settings underway. Namely, always check with the working navigator before making changes.

But beyond the display differences and variability, we need to adopt a new, more interactive approach to "chart reading." Unlike with paper charts or RNCs, where all the information is printed either on the chart or in the *Light List* and *U.S. Coast Pilot*, with ENCs much of this same broad range of information is included directly in the database, and we reveal this information by cursor picks of the objects themselves. In the example mentioned about the light on a tower, we would learn what the ENC knows about this light from a mouse-click on the light symbol—or some equivalent gesture such as rolling a cross hair on the chart to the location of the object.

Like any new technology, there is a learning curve, especially for those of us who grew up using paper charts. On the other hand, for those brand new to navigation, this is not so much a learning *curve*; it is more just learning how to do it.

To help with this, Chapter 2 addresses practical distinctions in the use of RNCs and ENCs, then in Chapter 3 we look at basic good practice for electronic chart navigation, and how this is adapted to the use of ENCs. In most cases this is just a matter of transitioning good practice from paper to computer screen.

1.4 ECDIS versus ECS

Now we confront a terminology challenge mariners face as they begin to use ENCs. The S-57 standard establishes what is in an ENC, but it does not specify how this information should be presented to the mariner in their specific electronic chart program. The IHO standard that covers how ENC data should be presented on the screen is called "S-52, Specifications for Chart Content and Display Aspects of ECDIS."

In other words, an S-57 chart (an ENC) is a database, that includes such information as the presence of a light at a specific Lat-Lon, how high it is, how bright it is, and so on, but the ENC itself does not specify what this light should look like on the display screen, nor does it tell us how we access specific data about that light. It is the S-52 standard that specifies the actual symbols to be used for various objects, and how they are to be displayed on the chart, along with what we obtain from a cursor pick, and how that cursor pick information should be presented.

But there is another key word in the title of the S-52 standard, namely "ECDIS." This acronym stands for Electronic Chart Display and Information Systems. An ECDIS is much more than an ECS. Recall that an ECS is *any* form of navigation software that can display echarts, usually with a GPS input and other basic navigation functions. An ECDIS, on the other hand, is an integrated system of software, sensors, and communications, each part of which must meet rigorous and specific performance and back-up standards set down by the International Maritime Organization (IMO).

The chart display aspects of S-52 are just one part of the full requirements of an IMO certified ECDIS. (IMO and IHO standards for ECDIS are published in a series of doc-

> "It may be noted that electronic chart systems not meeting these ECDIS specifications of IHO and IMO, or ECDIS using non-official data, are known as ECS (Electronic Chart Systems)."
>
> **— S-52, Section 1.2 (a)**

uments.) We could have, for example, an ECS that met all of the chart display standards of S-52, and yet not at all be allowed to describe itself as ECDIS, because there are so many other requirements to be met for what is called "type approved ECDIS."

In addition to the hardware, integrated communications, back-up requirements, and alarm protocols for ECDIS, there are also specific requirements for how the navigation software itself must function that go far beyond just chart display standards.

In this book, we concentrate on the chart symbols and chart data presentation and do not focus on other aspects of the navigation programs showing them. And, indeed, we are mainly addressing users of ECS programs that do not meet the full ECDIS standards. Mariners using type-approved ECDIS are required to undergo extensive training in its use, which is another distinction between ECS and ECDIS.

But even though most ECS software in use today by mariners worldwide do not meet ECDIS standards, the S-52 specification is the governing international standard they have to work with when presenting chart data. Consequently, ECS programs capable of showing ENCs do indeed use the S-52 standard as a guide to presenting the ENC data. Many follow it very closely, others differ in only insignificant ways, and still other manufacturers decide their users are better off with some variation of the standard.

For example, in an ENC, every object on the chart and its attributes have unique 6-letter acronyms (codes), but the S-52 specification states that objects and attributes should be identified in "human readable language," which seems to imply not by acronyms alone. Some ECS programs adhere to that guidance, others do not. Some ECS use both acronyms and plain language, as many ECDIS do, which seems a good solution.

Likewise, some symbols are S-52 specified to use a line thickness that is twice as thick as used on other symbols, or some symbols are intended to be a slightly different color when conspicuous versus not conspicuous. Again, some ECS programs follow these guides and others do not, but in both cases we

still learn the crucial information from a cursor pick of the object. In other words, the presentations are not quite uniform in ECS, but they are rarely distracting.

Occasionally, we might run across a presentation that is not consistent with S-52 that could be distracting. There are crucial aspects of the presentation that must be understood and should be consistent for safe, efficient navigation. A goal of this book is to provide the background on that structure that is needed to extract all the crucial information possible from an ENC. The S-52 chart display standard in action is a primary focus of this book.

1.5 ENC Names and Boundaries

When procuring and organizing our RNCs, we find they are identical to the paper charts they are copies of. Electronic or paper, they have the same names and boundaries. This changes when we move into the world of ENCs.

Suppose you want to look at the ENC equivalent of RNC 18465, Strait of Juan de Fuca, Eastern Part. You will find this chart on the NOAA Interactive Catalog, ENC section (see References). The chart number is US4WA34M, and it is indeed described on the NOAA site as equivalent to 18465, Strait of Juan de Fuca, Eastern part. The actual ENC coverage, however, is shown in Figure 1.5-1.

ENC chart US4WA34M (the blue part alone in Figure 1.5-1) does not at all cover the same waters as its equivalent RNC, 18465. If you want all the ENC charting that covers the waters of 18465 you will need 9 ENCs, with a baffling distribution of borders. They are mostly rectilin-

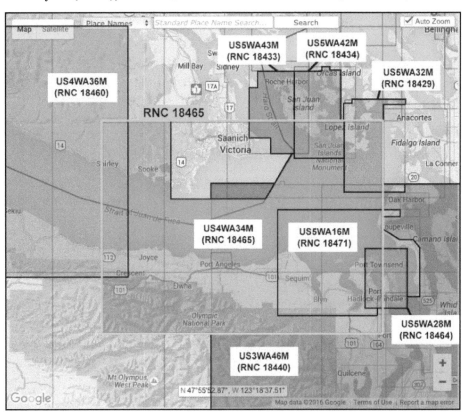

Figure 1.5-1. *ENC boundaries in the vicinity of paper chart (RNC) 18465 (turquoise outline), along the northern border of the U.S. with Canada.*

ear boundaries, though not in a single rectangle. This is true for most ENCs worldwide. The only exception here is one side of the completely missing area around the Canadian town of Victoria, BC, which we will come back to.

Also, the scales of adjacent charts do not match in the same way many RNCs do. With RNCs, we often have a sequence of neighboring charts on the same scale, but this is not always the case with the ENCs. Chart 18465 is 1:80,000; the scales of the ENCs that covers the area of 18465 vary from 1:20,000 to 1:100,000.

With ENCs, however, the display disruption going between adjacent charts of differing scales is not as often an issue as it can be in some RNC displays, so these scale differences are not a distraction.

The irregularities in borders and scales stem from the IHO standards for ENCs, which, among other restrictions, prevent any overlap of adjacent charts of the same scale band—in contrast to RNCs, which usually overlap. The only overlap allowed is when one cell (another name for an ENC) is fully included within another cell of a smaller scale band. In Figure 1.5-1, US5WA16M and US5WA28M overlap US3WA46M, but no others overlap, and the former two do not overlap each other.

This brings us to a key concept in understanding the boundaries and naming of ENCs, namely the concept of *scale band,* also called *usage band.* The IHO defines six usage bands, and recommends the scale ranges that each of these bands should cover. U.S. scale bands are listed in Table 1.5-1 and compared to others in Table 1.5-2. These definitions are useful for selecting charts in catalogs, for understanding the chart names, and in turn, the ENC boundaries we see in navigation programs. The larger the scale band, the larger the chart scale.

The U.S. scale ranges do not coincide with the IHO recommendations, which are the same as the UK values shown in Table 1.5-2, because the U.S. has been making ENCs before the IHO made their recommendations. The scale band is key to understanding the names of all ENCs.

The first two letters of an ENC name identify the hydrographic office (HO) responsible for the chart (Appendix A2). The digit following the HO identifier is the scale band. For example, US4WA34M, the "US4" is part of the international prefix to the chart, meaning a U.S. (NOAA) product, of scale band 4 (i.e. between 1:50,000 and 1:150,000). Everything after the "US4" is the actual name of the chart assigned by the HO that made it, NOAA in this case. In the NOAA chart naming system, the "WA" means the chart is either wholly within the state of Washington, or, when spanning adjacent states, the majority of the chart is in the state of Washington. Scale bands 3 to 6 are generally associated with a specific state. Bands 1 and 2 are often labeled: EC (for East Coast), GC (for Gulf Coast), and WC (for West Coast), but there are some overlaps in these descriptors with the state descriptors.

We can think of the "M" used on NOAA ENCs as a reminder that the native units of these charts are metric (although we can display them in other units if we choose), or we can think of it as a filler, because all ENC names worldwide must be eight characters long—dealing with an extra M is probably better than dealing with leading zeros.

The fact that the actual sequence of numbers in the ENC names (i.e., the "34" in the sample being discussed) do not always follow a logical sequence along a waterway, is just a matter of history in the production sequence, much as RNC chart numbers are not in any particularly logical order—ENCs are often more in sequence than their RNC counterparts. In a few cases, NOAA ENC chart numbers include letters, i.e., US4AK5PM.

Thus we have this sequence of charts coming in from the ocean toward San Francisco:

Table 1.5-2 Scale Bands Compared*				
	NOAA	*UKHO*	*CHS*	*U.S. PAPER*
2,000,000	US1	GB1	CA1	SAILING
1,500,000	US2			
600,000		GB2		
500,000	US3		CA2	GENERAL
350,000		GB3		
150,000				
90,000	US4		CA3	COASTAL
75,000		GB4		
50,000				
30,000	US5		CA4	
22,000				HARBOR
20,000		GB5		
5,000			CA5	
4,000	US6			
2,000		GB6	CA6	

*Example: A 1:40,000 ENC would be scale band 5 in the U.S., but would be labeled scale band 4 on charts produced by the Canadian Hydrographic Service (CHS).

Table 1.5-1 Scale Bands for ENC				
Scale Band	Usage Band	NOAA ENC		
1	Overview	Smaller than		1:1,500,000
2	General	1:600,000	to	1:1,500,000
3	Coastal	1:150,000	to	1:600,000
4	Approach	1:50,000	to	1:150,000
5	Harbor	1:5,000	to	1:50,000
6	Berthing	Larger than		1:5,000

US1WC01M (1:3,500,000)

US2WC12M (1: 1,200,000)

US2WC06M (1: 811,980)

US2WC05M (1:868,003)

US3CA14M (1:207,840)

US5CA12M (1:40,000)

US5CA13M (1:20,000)

The best way to learn of available charts is NOAA's online Interactive Chart Viewer (Figure 1.5-2), or the IHO counterpart for global coverage, discussed in the next section. NOAA ENC chart numbers are only unique within state designations and scale bands. Thus there is a US5WA16M (Approaches to Admiralty Inlet, Dungeness to Oak Bay) as well as a US5FL16M (St.Marks River and Approaches), but there are never two charts with the identical full name.

In learning to use this system, we might also keep in mind that the U.S. ENC scale bands are not the same as those that have historically been used in the U.S. for paper chart scale categories (Table 1.5-2), as defined in Chapter 1 of any *U.S. Coast Pilot* and in *Bowditch*.

Finally, we return to the diagonal border line noted in Figure 1.5-1 at the top of this section. That rare situation stems from another IHO standard related to adjacent national borders. Two nations cannot each make an ENC of the same waters, so some agreement must be made between nations as to who covers overlapping waterways. There is no such restriction in paper charts, where we often have the same waters covered by charts from different nations.

In this case, Canada maintained the right for that section of the waterway, and offers chart CA470075 for those waters, which identifies it as Canadian (CA), scale band 4, and chart number 70075. The unique situation this presents Pacific Northwest mariners is, a U.S. vessel navigating by free U.S. ENCs, leaving Haro Strait bound for, say, Port Angeles, must either switch to an RNC for this section, or purchase this one Canadian ENC, which entails chart registration as well as computer authorization for just this one chart. On the other hand, the global standards set down by the IHO solve tremendously more international charting conflicts than the very few disruptions like this that they might cause.

1.6 Sources of ENC

As noted, one of the advantages of ENCs is the ability to update them with small correction files that can be downloaded with an internet connection, or even by an email attachment over satellite phone without a broadband connection underway.

The ability to do this more or less automatically within an ECS is one of the formal ECDIS requirements that is nicely implemented in many popular ECS programs, though not necessarily in the specific form required by ECDIS. Many navigation programs can be configured to check for latest editions of all charts you have installed with a button click, or automatically each time the program starts. Some ECS programs include convenient ways to select and download worldwide ENCs as well.

Without a built-in option, charts can be manually updated from the primary producing agency or authorized

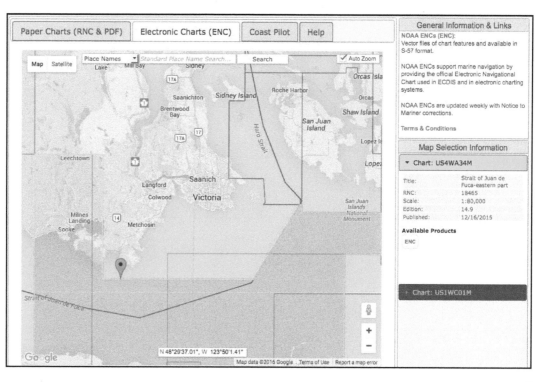

Figure 1.5-2. *NOAA's convenient interactive index to ENCs and RNCs. Red borders mark NOAA charts. The selected one changes to yellow with its information on the right. The marker shows the place you clicked. Note the missing U.S. ENC coverage south of Victoria, BC despite U.S. coverage on all sides.*

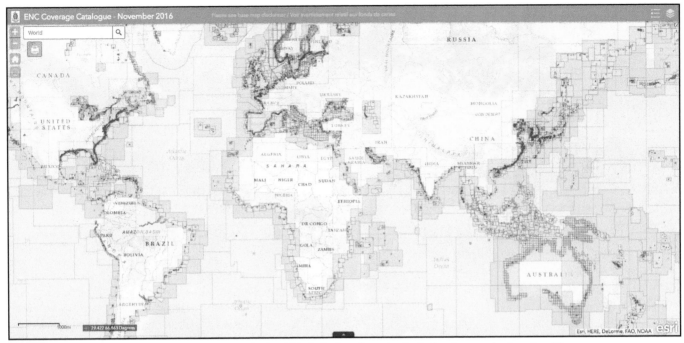

Figure 1.6-1. *IHO's interactive global index to ENCs. This is for locating charts, but not a way to download them.*

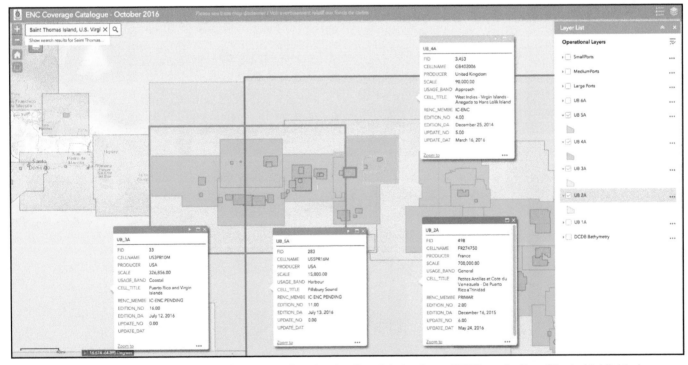

Figure 1.6-2. *Annotated detail from the IHO chart catalog showing the global nature of ENC production. Charts highlighted are from UK, U.S., and FR. We have added and color coded several cursor pick reports, which usually show only one at a time. v*

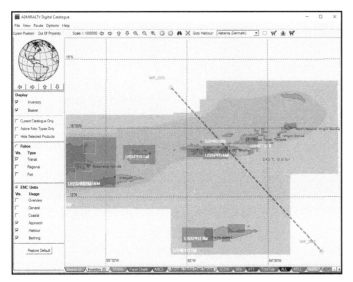

Figure 1.6-3. *The UKHO's Admiralty Digital Catalog PC app for chart selection and ordering. It will prepare an order for all products along a selected route.*

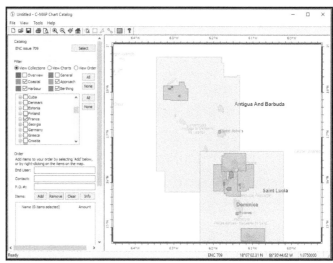

Figure 1.6-4. *C-Map offers authorized global ENC coverage. Their catalog app has several convenient features including a way to show only charts from a particular HO.*

outlet. NOAA charts have a convenient online interactive catalog at nauticalcharts.noaa.gov, with graphic and tabular indexes. Charts can be downloaded individually or by regions. Other nations have similar online services, including convenient interactive catalogs.

The IHO global catalog of ENCs can be found at www. iho.int under "ENC Availability" (click the image). See Figures 1.6-1 and 1.6-2. The IHO site also has a list of all "Online Chart Catalogs." The UKHO pioneered the interactive catalog as a way to identify needed products (publications, printed charts, RNCs, and ENCs) along with a way to prepare an order that can be emailed to a chart agent. Their product is a PC app called Admiralty Digital Catalog. With it a user can lay out a route and obtain a report of all hydrographic products that relate to locations along the route, including a list of the ENCs, not just from the UK, but all official sources (Figure 1.6-3).

Several private companies including C-Map (Figure 1.6-4) and Primar in Norway offer IHO authorized global ENC coverage, along with convenient interactive catalogs for both chart selection and purchase.

An automated chart selection from within your ECS with your choice of source is typically the easiest way to install ENCs; working with full regions rather than individual charts simplifies the process. When we do choose to install charts manually, it helps to understand what is involved, because this is also taking place when we do it automatically.

With the manual approach to ENC installation we download the files to our computers, usually as compressed zip-files, named with the chart or region name, which in turn contain a folder named ENC_ROOT.

The ENC_ROOT folder contains a CATALOG.031 file, several text files, and a folder with the name of the chart. The text files here describe the chart, but are not part of it. The chart folder includes the base chart (ENC *cell*) with extension .000, and several other text files that are indeed part of the chart. Updates to this chart cell will then be named with extensions .001, .002, etc. These do not replace the .000 file, they are added to the series of such cells that are accessed when you open that ENC in your ECS program.

The CATALOG.031 file within the ENC_ROOT folder describes the package just downloaded (called an *exchange set*), in this example a single chart. This important file specifies all the ENC cells and ancillary files needed by the chart or charts within the set. The extension ".031" is named after the version of S-57 used in the production of the charts, which at present is Edition 3.1, dated November, 2000. The file structure is:

USWA21M.zip →
  ENC_ROOT
      CATALOG.031
      README.TXT
      USERAGREEMENT.TXT
      US5WA21M
         US5WA21A.TXT
         US5WA21B.TXT
         US5WA21M.000

Introduction to Electronic Chart Navigation

When a full region is downloaded, the file structure is similar. Here is an example of the download option of all charts in the state of Washington (WA):

WA_ENC.zip →

ENC_ROOT

CATALOG.031

README.TXT

US5WA21M

US5WA21M

US5WA21M...

The total list is 73 charts, with each chart folder including files similar to the single chart example above. The CATALOG.031 file in this case describes what is expected for all 73 of the charts in this exchange set. (These 73 ENCs, by the way, were delivered in a single ZIP file of 39 MB, which is the size of about 5 RNCs.)

We can see immediately why most ECS programs encourage downloading full regions rather than individual charts; we are dealing with folders (ENC_ROOT) and files (CATALOG.031) that have the same name, but different and crucial content with each download. This is also in part why chart dealers sell ENCs in full, large geographic regions rather than individually—though there is obviously a commercial aspect to that decision as well, and we can indeed find some outlets that will sell individual ENCs. This also accounts in part for why the auto-update function of many ECS programs only functions for full regions. Charts installed individually have to be updated manually.

Note the phrase "chart dealers *sell* ENC" just mentioned. Navigators in U.S. waters are extremely lucky when it comes to electronic charts, because, first, NOAA produces very high quality charts updated weekly, and second, they are free. This becomes more extraordinary the more we learn about charts from other nations, which are expensive—and it is an ongoing expense, essentially a subscription that must be renewed every year or two. These charts are expensive to produce, maintain, and distribute. (As a historical note, NOAA started out selling their electronic charts, but that system ended in December, 2001.)

What we have to face is this: once a computer file is to be sold, it has to be copy protected, and that adds a layer of complexity to ENC use outside of U.S. waters. Beyond the commercial need to protect charts being sold, we hear arguments that charts must be encrypted to guarantee their authenticity, but that is much like manufacturers of heavy bronze sextants arguing that professional navigators prefer the inertia of hefty instruments over equally accurate aluminum alloys. The unprotected ENC from NOAA are arguably the best in the world, they are updated weekly, and used without question by shipping companies worldwide.

The IHO certified system of encryption used for ENCs is given in the *S-63, IHO Data Protection Scheme.* Thus an "S-63 chart" is the encrypted form of the equivalent "S-57 chart" (unencrypted ENC). When we purchase international ENCs from a hydrographic office or authorized outlet, they will be delivered in the S-63 format. To display these, we first need an ECS that is capable of displaying S-63 charts. Not all programs capable of showing S-57 charts can show S-63 charts without the addition of a special option or plug-in to do so. Authorizing an ECS to display S-63 charts will certify a specific ECS program, running on a specific computer, often with the option to have one back-up installation on another system.

The procedures for authorizing your computer and registering S-63 charts with a hydrographic office vary from one ECS to another and from one chart source to another. The first time through, the process might seem complex, but done once, it is usually fairly fast and efficient going forward.

Nevertheless, large international shipping companies that must use encrypted charts from several nations do often choose to purchase NOAA charts that have been encrypted by a third party so that all charts on the vessel use the same S-63 system from the same chart source and use the same updating procedures. Likewise, recreational mariners often use commercial ECS programs in computers or tablets that simplify the chart organization by incorporating the NOAA charts into their own encrypted chart packages.

The computer file structure and exchange set packages are essentially the same for S-57 and S-63 charts, but the latter will be stored in a separate directory and will include a few special files to handle the security and registration. However, when it comes to actually viewing an ENC, the primary cell files (name.000, name.001, name.002) are handled by the ECS in the same manner, which always involves an intermediate step.

SENC files

The primary ENC cell files discussed above are not the actual source of data displayed on the screen by the ECS. When we open an ENC for the first time, the ECS program reads the primary files (original and updates) and from these files it creates an entirely new database in a format unique to each ECS, which is called the System ENC, or SENC file. This file is then stored on the computer in a specific, but generally not identified location. There is no need for users to interact with those files on any level, but these are indeed the actual data files being read and displayed on the screen. If you get an update to the chart, the SENC file will be updated but that is behind scene.

Thus the ENC cell files (name.000, etc) are identical on everyone's ECS, but the SENC files are unique to the specific ECS brand. The only practical implication of this process is the total file size stored. ENC are relatively small files (never larger than 5 Mb), and their updates are even smaller, which is a big advantage when downloading them over, say, a satellite phone connection at sea; but once the ENC has been displayed on the screen, the total file size stored for that ENC is roughly twice the size of the download, because SENC files are about the same size as the primary files they are made from.

1.7 What is on an ENC chart?

Things depicted on an ENC chart are called *objects*. Objects can be areas, lines, or points. The areas may or may not be defined by visible lines, and a line object can be short segments, or long lines, either dashed or solid, symbolized or plain. Point objects are marked by chart symbols.

Every single thing we see on an ENC is an object, or more precisely, a stack of overlapping objects. A buoy is a point object on top a depth area object, on top of a named sea area object, on top of a navigational system of marks area object (IALA B). If we cursor pick that buoy symbol we will be told all of that, plus more in many cases.

All objects in an ENC, including how each is to be specified, is all very precisely prescribed by the S-57 standard. A few examples of ENC objects are given in Table 1.7-1. The full list (178 at last count) is in Appendix A3. All objects have a unique six-letter acronym, and although relying on these acronyms in the ENC presentation to the mariner is discouraged in the S-52 standard, they can be helpful when discussing the charts.

Specific objects can also be presented in more than one geometric form. For example, the object *lateral buoy* (BOYLAT) or object *lights* (LIGHTS) are aways point objects, but the object *land area* (LNDARE) could be a point, a line, or an area. The object *land elevation* (LNDELV) can be a line or a point, corresponding to an elevation contour or a spot elevation.

The meanings of most objects are clear from their short descriptions, but what all a specific object class includes

is not always obvious. Towers, for example, are not an ENC charted object; they are included within the object landmark (LNDMRK). Likewise, ENCs do not have lighted buoys, they have lights and they have buoys. In an ENC these are separate objects. Even the topmark on a buoy is a separate object.

Each object has a prescribed set of *attributes* that are used to define or characterize the object in its present context. The same attribute can be used to describe various objects, and an attribute that may be used with a specific object might not be included on all such objects on the same ENC. Some attributes are mandatory, others are optional if known. For example, many objects can have an attribute *object name* (OBJNAM), but not all do, whereas every light object must have an attribute *light characteristic* (LITCHR). A tower shown on the chart would be encoded as object *landmark* (LNDMRK) with attribute *category of landmark* (CATLMK) = "tower." A short list of attribute examples is shown in Table 1.7-2, with the full list (last count 182) given in Appendix A4. Attributes also have acronyms, as just illustrated.

Attributes can be assigned a numerical value, a selection from a specified category list, or a text string unique to that object. An object *lights* (LIGHTS), for example, could have, among other attributes, an attribute *height* (HEIGHT) = "23 m"; an attribute *light characteristic* (LITCHR) = "Interrupted Quick Flashing," (which is #9, from a specific list), and an attribute *object name* (OBJNAM) = "Fourmile Rock Light."

We might pause a moment to highlight the "terminology challenge" mentioned at the start of Section 1.4. That originally referred to distinguishing between ECDIS and ECS, and between S-57 and S-52. Now we extend the challenge. There is good reason the S-52 standard discourages

Table 1.7-1. Examples of S-57 OBJECTS*	
Object acronym	*Description*
BOYLAT	Buoy, lateral
DPAREA	Depth area
LIGHTS	Light
LNDARE	Land area
LNDMRK	Landmark
SBDARE	Seabed area
SLCONS	Shoreline Construction
TOPMAR	Topmark
UWTROC	Underwater/awash rock
VEGATN	Vegetation

* See Appendix A3 for a full list.

Table 1.7-2. Examples of S-57 ATTRIBUTES*	
Attribute acronym	*Description*
BOYSHP	Buoy shape
CATFOG	Category of fog signal
CATLMK	Category of landmark
CATVEG	Category of vegetation
COLOR	Color
COLPAT	Color pattern
CONVIS	Conspicuous visually
EXPSOU	Exposition of sounding
HEIGHT	Height
LITCHR	Light characteristic
LNDELV	Land elevation
NATSUR	Nature of surface
VALSOU	Value of sounding
WATLEV	Water level effect

* See Appendix A4 for a full list.

use of acronyms alone. Both object and attribute acronyms are six letters, always in caps. CATWEB, for example, is an *attribute* (category of weed or kelp) of the *object* WED-KLP (weed or kelp). No navigator should ever be expected to know that; but if questions come up about chart specifications, it can help to know the conventions used and have a place in mind to look this up. Even the names of the standards are a challenge to keep straight—without having spoken them out loud a number of times in various contexts!

S-57 specifies what is in the ENC.

S-52 specifies how the ENC should be presented.

Both standards are available online in full (see References); the discussion in this book relates to both. We can be certain that any ENC we use follows the S-57 standard (that is a definition); but when using an ECS to view the ENC, as opposed to official ECDIS, the S-52 display standards are sometimes approximated or compromised.

At the end of this section there are two annotated examples of how a few common objects are presented, noting aspects that might not be anticipated by paper chart navigators. A key to the fullest use of ENCs is knowing what all we might know about any specific object. In other words, what are the prescribed attributes for each object, and how are these defined?

The primary reference for these details is *S-57 Appendix A: Part 1, Object Catalog* and *Part 2, Attribute Catalog* (see References), which could be downloaded to the navigation computer for further reference.

Alternatively, the online service from Teledyne CARIS offers a very convenient depiction of S-57 objects and attributes at

www.caris.com/s-57 .

This interactive presentation unravels the complex interplay between attributes and objects, and makes it easy to learn which attributes apply to which objects, along with

Table 1.7-3. Samples of S-57 ATTRIBUTE CATEGORIES*			
CATVEG**	**CATLMK**	**NATSUR**	**WATLEV**
grass	cairn	mud	partly submerged at high water
bush	cemetery	clay	always dry
deciduous wood	chimney	silt	always underwater/submerged
coniferous wood	dish aerial	sand	covers and uncovers
wood in general	flagstaff (flagpole)	stone	awash
mangroves	flare stack	gravel	subject to inundation or flooding
mixed crops	mast	pebbles	floating
reed	windsock	cobbles	
moss	monument	marsh	**EXPSOU**
tree in general	column (pillar)	lava	within the range of depth of the surrounding depth area
evergreen tree	memorial plaque	coral	shoaler than the range of depth of the surrounding depth area
coniferous tree	obelisk	shells	deeper than the range of depth of the surrounding depth area
palm tree	statue	boulder	
nipa palm tree	cross		**CONVIS**
casuarina tree	dome	**CATFOG**	visually conspicuous
eucalypt tree	radar scanner	explosive	not visually conspicuous
deciduous tree	tower	diaphone	
mangrove tree	windmill	siren	**COLPAT**
filao tree	windmotor	nautophone	horizontal stripes
	spire/minaret	reed	vertical stripes
	large rock or boulder on land	tyfon	diagonal stripes
		bell	squared
		whistle	stripes (direction unknown)
		gong	border stripe
		horn	

* For an online catalog showing all values possible for all attributes, see www.caris.com/s-57.

** See Table 1.7-2

the definitions of the attribute categories (samples are shown in Table 1.7-3). In principle, this type of interactive presentation could be included in an ECS or ECDIS program, but we have not seen it done.

Cursor Pick Reports

Chart reading on an ENC is an interactive process, a step into modernization of navigation. On a paper chart we see all there is to know from the chart by looking at it. Looking at an ENC, we see only a fraction of the information it includes. In numerous cases, we must click the chart just to learn what we would know at a glance from the corresponding paper chart—but then, almost certainly, learning a lot more. We might compare a person sitting motionlessly reading a traditional printed book to someone reading an illustrated ebook in an electronic device. The latter is likely panning and zooming images for the best display, highlighting sections, clicking words to look up their meanings, book marking, adding notes, and so on. Modern ENC reading now is done as much with the hands (on a mouse or track ball) as with the eyes.

When we click an object on an ENC (a cursor pick) we get back a list of all objects at that point (a pick report), along with sublists of all the attributes that apply to each object. How this report is formatted and displayed on the screen depends on the ECS in use. In fact, it also depends on the ECDIS in use, because this display varies among all navigation programs. We can be certain that a type-approved ECDIS will include *all* the possible data, whereas most ECS choose edit the list of objects and attributes on some level. There can be a dozen or more object layers on some pick reports, not all of which are crucial to typical navigation concerns.

ECS pick reports appear in one of three formats, they use acronyms only, acronyms and plain language, or plain language only. A sample of the latter is shown in Table 1.7-4 for the cursor pick of a lighted buoy, showing all the underlying layers that we might see—the image of the buoy was added. Symbols are sometimes shown in pick reports, but not often. The objects and attributes shown are discussed later in the book.

Cursor pick examples

There are more practical details in Chapter 2, but for an introduction to what we can learn from an ENC, we look at the cursor pick of the light shown in Figure 1.7-1. The results are presented in Table 1.7-5 with annotations. When we cursor pick that light symbol we get a list of everything located at that point. There is a prescribed order, but that order is not always followed by all ECS; in any event, we usually get all the key information. In this discussion we are looking at the top four objects, namely a light, a beacon, a fog signal, and the land these are sitting on.

Notice that each of the three point objects has its own symbol (a flare, a thin rectangle, and a sound wave symbol). If you carefully made the cursor pick on any one of

---

Table 1.7-4 Sample Pick Report*

US5VA20M	36° 58.26' N, 076° 06.297' W
Buoy, lateral	
Shape	Pillar
Category	Port-hand lateral mark
Color	Green
Name	Thimble Shoal Channel Lighted Buoy 7
Light	
Color	Green
Exhibition condition	Night light
Characteristic	Flashing
Group	(1)
Period	2.5 s
Sequence	00.3+(02.2)
Restricted area	
Information	Regulated navigation area, 33 CFR165.501: Navigation regulations are published in Chapter 2 of the U.S U.S. Coast Pilot for this geographic area.
Restriction	Entry restricted
Navigational system of marks	
Marks system	IALA B
Fairway	
Name	Thimble Shoal Channel
Traffic	Two-way
Magnetic variation	
Reference year	2015
Annual change	-1'
Variation	-11°
Quality of data	
Zone of confidence	A1
Source date	20110800
Text description:	US5VA20D.TXT
Depth area	
Contours	10.9 m - 36.5 m
Dredged area	
Sounding	14.5 m
Name	Thimble Shoal Channel LOQ
Nautical publication information	
Usage	Harbour
Compilation Scale	20000
Source date	20110800
Source	US,US,graph,Chart 12254
Text description	US5VA20A.TXT

* This is an example of clicking an object where a lot is going on at that location, ten layers of objects. Objects and attributes shown in this report are explained in later sections.

them, away from their overlapping center point, you could get (depending on the ECS) a report for just that object plus the land under it. This behavior is important to remember because, unlike RNCs, when we zoom into an ENC, it is only the line and area objects that zoom; point objects, i.e., the chart symbols, remain at their specified sizes, which are pretty small on some screens. Also the fog signal (sound wave) symbol color is specified as magenta, which is not very prominent when shown on top of tan land or a water shade, and this varies with the ambient lighting. Thus we might click a light hoping to learn all about it, but miss the fog signal. (We see later that ECS programs do not all respond to cursor picks of related objects like these in the same manner.)

The pick report tells us all that is in the ENC for these objects, but we must rely on our own experience with ENCs, or a list of attributes, to learn what might be known but is not given. In this example we learn what we would most likely need about this light, but there could be more, meaning valid attributes of the object that are not known. This light, for example, has a name according to the *Canadian Light List*, so it could have the attribute *object name* (OBJNAM) of "Race Rocks Light," but that is not given. More practically, we could want to know if this light is on during the daytime. That would be the attribute *exhibition condition of light* (EXCLIT), which can be: always on, daytime only, fog only, or night only. At this point in time, that is not known for this light.

Looking at Figure 1.7-2 and the beacon report in Table 1.7-5, we see more that could usefully be included in the ENC. This is a conspicuous object, meaning the attribute *visually conspicuous* (CONVIS) is clearly applicable. CONVIS does not apply to object LIGHTS, but it does apply to beacons, and it is not there in this case. Also this light is in both the U.S. and the Canadian Light Lists, so

it would be nice to have both Light List numbers. Other lights along this shared waterway do have both.

Indeed, this object (Figure 1.7-2) could be identified in the ENC as an object *landmark* (LNDMRK), both historically and visually. The object LNDMRK could then have attribute *category of landmark* (CATLMK) = "tower"; attribute *function* (FUNCTN) = "light support"; attribute *vertical length* (VERLEN) = "80 ft." And then those, along with attribute *visually conspicuous* (CONVIS) = "yes" could be applied to the beacon object.

In short, a virtue of the ENC is that the format is all in place to add new information about any of the charted objects. The symbols are not going to change, they are fixed in both size and design, but the characterization of the object and the list of attributes can expand to cover more of what we would learn from the *Light List*, *U.S. Coast Pilot*, or local knowledge. However, despite not having reached full potential with this symbol's description, the ENC still provides much more information than does the RNC for the same light.

For completeness, we might note that even though this light tower was not listed as a landmark, we do get some hint of its value to navigation from the beacon symbol itself. Within ENC terms, towers, prominent lattice structures, and large pile structures are called *major beacons*, whereas stakes and poles are called *minor beacons*. Major and minor beacons have slightly different symbols, as shown in Figure 1.7-3. They are similar, but noting this adds to chart reading skill. Minor beacon symbols are thinner and taller. This is an example of the interplay between the S-52 and S-57 standards. The ENC (S-57) does not specify a beacon as major or minor, but S-52 specifies a major or minor beacon symbol depending on the value of its beacon shape attribute (BCNSHP).

Furthermore, S-52 specifies two styles of symbols be available to the user: one called "simplified," which we have been using so far, and one called "paper chart," which emulate those of traditional paper charts. The distinction between major and minor beacons is more prominent in the latter style (see insert to Figure 1.7-3). Optional symbol

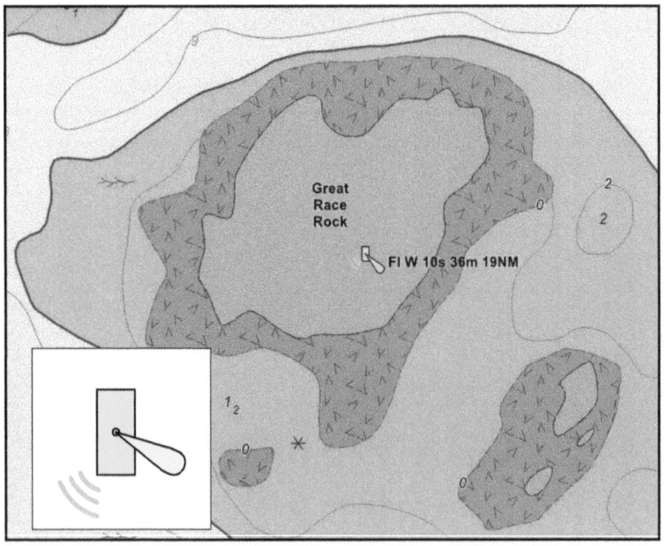

Figure 1.7-1. *ENC presentation of a lighted beacon with simplified symbols and light label showing. From CA570101.*

Figure 1.7-2. *Race Rocks Lighthouse was established in 1860 and manned until 1996.*

Object	Attribute	Displayed on screen		Notes
		Location	48° 17.881N, 123° 31.884 W	
LIGHTS		**Light**		
	COLOR	Color	White	#1 from a list of 13
	HEIGHT	Height	118.1 ft	Height above MHW
	INFORM	Information	PAC 189	Canadian Light List number
	LITCHR	Light characteristic	flashing	#2 from a list of 29
	SIGGRP	Signal group	(1)	All non-grouped lights use this.
	SIGPER	Signal period	10 seconds	Time over which the pattern repeats
	SIGSEQ	Signal sequence	00.3+(09.7)	Lighted+(eclipsed) in seconds
	VALNMR	Nominal range	19.2 nmi	
FOGSIG		**Fog signal**		
	CATFOG	Category	horn	#10 from a list of 10
	INFORM	Information	horn points 155°	A unique detail, not part of a list
	SIGGRP	Signal group	(3)	Sounds in groups of 3
	SIGPER	Signal period	60.0 seconds	Time over which the pattern repeats
	SIGSEQ	Signal sequence	2.0+(3.0)+2.0+(3.0)+2.0+(48.0)	Sounds+(silent) in seconds
	SCAMIN	Scale minimum	(40000)	Shows on chart scales ≥ 1:40,000
BCNSPP		**Beacon, special purpose/general**		
	BCNSHP	Beacon shape	beacon tower	#3 from a list of 7
	CATSPM	Category	general warning mark	#27 from a list of 56
	COLOR	Color	black, white, black, white, black	#1 and 2 from a list of 13
	COLPAT	Color pattern	horizontal stripes	#1 from a list of 6
LNDARE		**Land area**		On international charts there is an English and a national language name.
	OBJNAM	Name	Great Race Rock	

Table title: **Table 1.7-5 Sample Annotated Cursor Pick Report**

styles are discussed in Chapter 2 and illustrated in Chapter 4. There is extended discussion of lights in Section 2.9.

For another example of how object-attribute descriptions are used in ENCs, we look at how the "docks" on Pier 55 in Figure 1.7-4 are presented—and the first note is: docks was in quotes for a reason. With any chart that is a database of terms (i.e., an ENC), we have to be tidy with terminology, and according to official maritime glossaries, a dock or slip is the space *between* piers intended for mooring a vessel.

So I should have said "piers," and when we cursor pick the pier at Point A we get the report shown in the figure, telling us that this is an object *shoreline construction* (SL-CON), with attributes *category of shoreline construction*

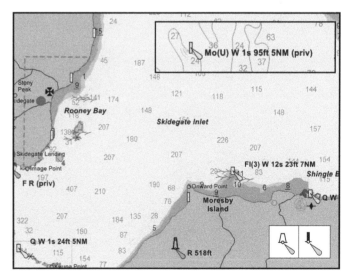

Figure 1.7-3. *Major and minor special purpose beacon symbols in the simplified symbols display. Major beacons are shorter and wider than minor. Either can occur with or without a light. The same applies to lateral beacons marking a waterway. Bottom right insert shows major minor beacon differences in the paper chart symbol style. On ENC, white lights have yellow flares. Lights with unknown color have the magenta flare.*

(CATSLC) = "pier," and attribute *water level effect* (WAT-LEV) = "always dry." So just as towers, domes, monuments, and such are no longer charted objects—they are categories of object *landmark* (LNDMRK)—we find now that piers, wharfs, breakwaters, sea walls, and such, are categories of object *shoreline construction* (SLCON). And a similar leeway is given the cartographer in how specific examples are to be described, which in turn can affect the symbols we see.

We do not see it so far, but in principle the ENC could distinguish between wharf and pier, where both are places to moor, but one extends into the water and the other does not. Furthermore, the object in Pick Report A is actually a floating dock, which on Canadian ENCs are all identified as the object *pontoon* (PONTON). The same object class is characterized by different conventions in the two separate hydrographic offices.

More importantly, note the subtlety of the thicker line segment being an actual (line) object, whereas a connecting thinner line is the border of a different object. Some ECS programs make this more prominent than others. Chapter 4 presents all ENC symbols, so these nuances can be studied there.

The point mentioned above comes up in several more places later in the book, namely ENCs from different hydrographic offices (nations) reveal different conventions on the encoding of their ENCs. All ENC production follows the same S-57 standard, but many of the prescriptions in that complex document offer optional solutions. It seems that each nation reads that document and then creates its own internal style sheet for how they will execute the declared options and undeclared ambiguities for their own products. There very few of these international differences, and mariners using charts from several nations will soon spot any significant examples and adapt to them.

1.8 NOAA ENC Online Viewer

As mentioned earlier, NOAA has a convenient online interface for graphically selecting and downloading ENC for all waters covered. A button click shows the corresponding RNC and PDF charts for download.

There is another ENC service from NOAA, however, that might be less known that is extremely valuable for learning about ENC, not to mention its efficacy for specific chart inquires. It is the NOAA ENC Online viewer that can be seen at

www.nauticalcharts.noaa.gov/ENCOnline .

You can view and interrogate all NOAA ENC this way, presented in a seamless (quilted) format and zoom in to view charts of larger scales. A sample is shown in Figure 1.8-1. With this viewer you display and interact with an ENC just as if you had it installed in an ECS that complied with the primary ECDIS display standards.

This is an ideal way to practice with ENCs and see the full range of attributes that can be learned from a cursor pick report. The viewer uses S-52 standards for symbology, and can you set depth contours and make other ECDIS standard display choices mentioned earlier and elaborated upon later in this book. Also if you know the name of a charted object (light, buoy, headland, bay...) anywhere in U.S. waters, you can search and find it, so long as that name has been encoded in the attribute *object name* (OBJNAM) on the chart it appears on. Likewise you can search for a specific ENC name, or for all, say, NY charts in scale band 5 using US5NY*, and so on. Beside training with ENCs as viewed in ECDIS, this can be a fast way to identify and confirm needed charts. Turn on the optional cell border display, find and check a chart of interest, then with the chart number in hand, go directly to the list of ENC by chart numbers to download it.

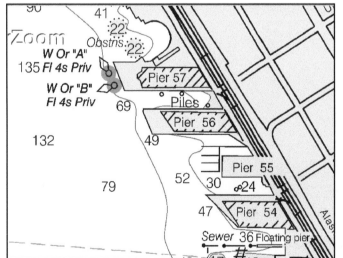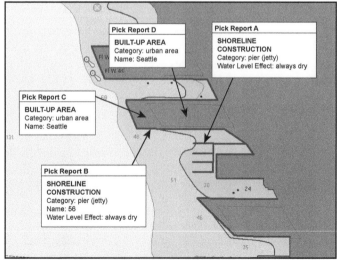

Figure 1.7-4. *Seattle waterfront as RNC (left) and ENC (right), with cursor pick points at several locations.*

Figure 1.8-1. *Sample screen from the NOAA online ENC viewer. Symbols follow closely the ECDIS standard as do the content of the pick reports, i.e., we see everything that is encoded at that location. Use of attribute acronyms alone is not standard, but these are all listed in Appendix 4. The sample shown has 12 layers of objects, which are accessed with the step button, top right. Typical display options and contour controls are present for a realistic ECDIS example of ENC viewing. Measurement tools and search options are included. The ENC cell outlines can also be shown to learn where charts are available. There is another sample of this viewer in Figure 2.13-1.*

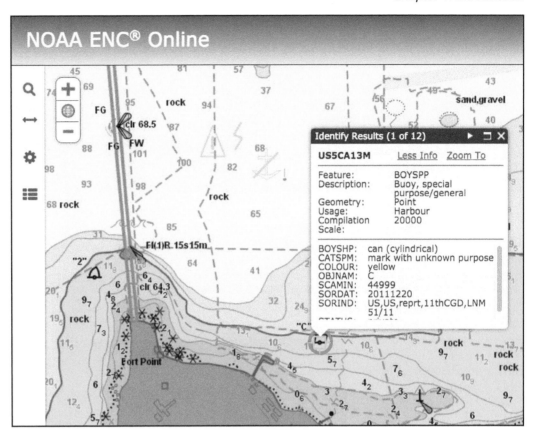

This service is also a way to quickly view any NOAA ENC without having to download and install the chart in your own ECS. Even with the RNC of a location in hand, this interactive view of the corresponding ENC can pro-vide more information about the chart and charted objects. Figure 1.8-2 shows a very informative feature of the NOAA Viewer that lets users overlay the ENC on any of a number of base maps.

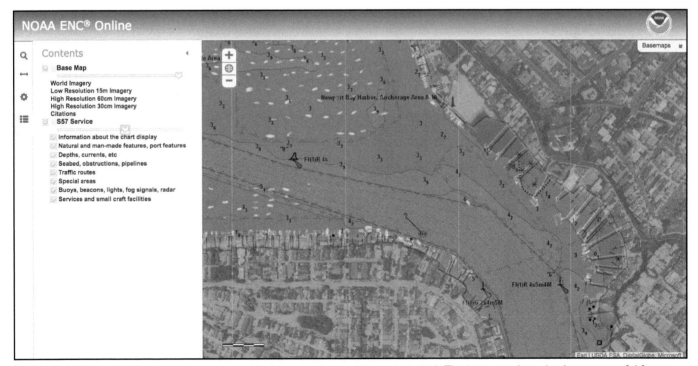

Figure 1.8-2.*Newport Beach ENC over a satellite image with transparency control. The topo map base is also very useful for understanding some charts. The transparency level of the ENC can be varied for the overlay.*

MACHC ENC Online

It would be wonderful to have such a convenient viewer for all ENCs worldwide, but there are numerous obstacles to that. Nevertheless, we can once again thank NOAA/OCS for their work with the IHO on a very exciting start in that direction. They share their ENC viewer technology with the MesoAmerican and Caribbean Sea Hydrographic Commission (MACHC) of the IHO, whose goal is to improve shipping and hydrographic communications across the region shown in Figure 1.8-3. Access to the MACHC ENC Online viewer and information on MACHC can be found at www.iho-machc.org.

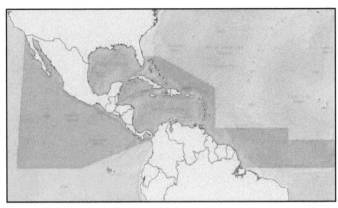

Figure 1.8-3. *Area of selected international charts that can be viewed in the MACHC ENC Online viewer.*

With the MACHC viewer, which functions just like the NOAA counterpart, you can see many selected charts from several nations, including some U.S. NGA charts not listed in the NOAA online catalog. You can, for example, take a detailed chart tour of the Panama Canal, or view Mexican, Cuban, and Colombian coasts on their own charts.

We see some charts that are not as detailed as typical NOAA charts, but part of the Commission goal is to work toward more uniform ENC coverage. On the other hand, we see high quality (attribute *zone of confidence* = "A1") Venezuelan ENC that even include elevation contours and roads that are missing from NOAA ENC (Figure 1.8-4). The UK and France are members of MACHC, but they do not seem to share their many fine ENCs in this region with this public viewer.

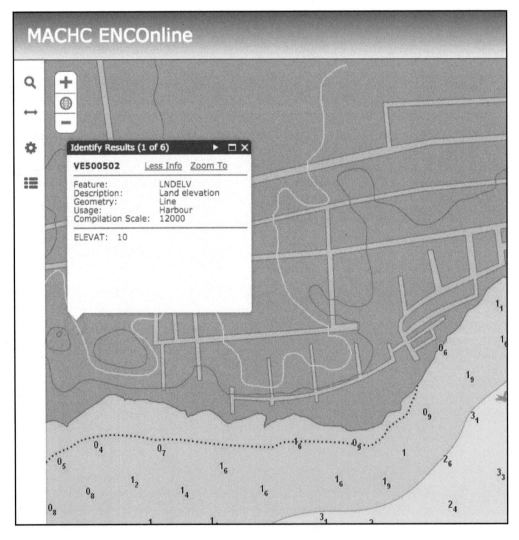

Figure 1.8-4. *A Venezuelan ENC on display in the MACHC viewer that shows elevation contours and roads, which are not seen on many ENC. Later we look into why many ENC do not include these contours with more discussion of this example. This viewer, which is the same as the NOAA ENC viewer, has the convenient feature of highlighting the boundaries of any object selected on the chart.*

Chapter 2

Key Distinctions Between ENC and RNC

2.1 Introduction

We have already covered several generic differences between raster navigational charts (RNCs) and the corresponding electronic navigational charts (ENCs), such as file sizes, nomenclature and boundaries, obtaining crucial content by cursor pick, and their respective places in nautical chart evolution. In this chapter we look into details that affect our usage of ENCs, focusing on the changes RNC users face when transitioning to ENC usage.

One notable difference is when ENCs are zoomed, only the land and water areas change size. Individual chart symbols stay the same size, specified in the S-52 standard (see Figure 2.1-1). This can appear counterintuitive to RNC users at first, but it becomes more understandable with practice. This feature leads to a cleaner display of a congested region of a chart when zoomed, but it remains the user's obligation to keep in mind the limitations of over-zooming discussed later.

The primary philosophical difference between RNCs and ENCs is the variability of ENC appearance. That they are notably different looking charts to begin with is not so much a challenge as the fact that the appearance of any one ENC can change. We are

accustomed to the invariance of RNCs. They pretty much look the same from one to the other, and any one of them never changes as we use it. This has been the policy in nautical charting for a hundred years. ENCs, on the other hand, purport the virtue of user customization of the chart display, and we look at these options in following sections.

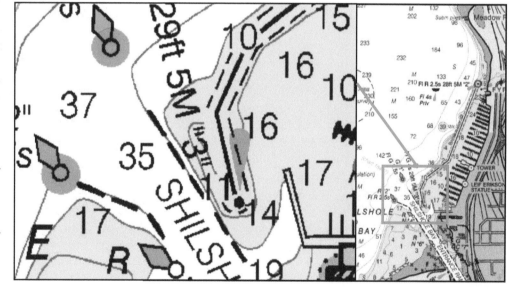

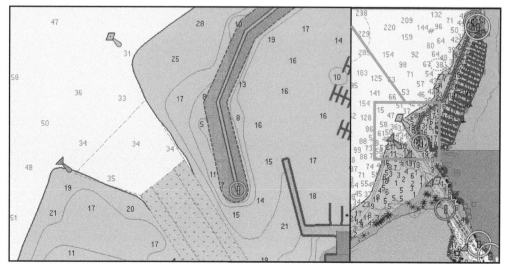

Figure 2.1-1. *Right side shows1:25,000 chart segments viewed at x1; on the left, each is zoomed to x6. Top is an RNC; bottom is the same chart as ENC. Symbol and text sizes do not change in the ENC.*

The most conspicuous content difference between RNC and ENC is absence of terrain detail on an ENC, which (at present) rarely contain elevation contours, roads, and other structures on the land part of the charts. This issue is addressed in Section 2.10. It is an example of the value of having both RNC and ENC formats installed.

2.2 Optional Display Modes

Both RNCs and ENCs offer color palette options for daylight, dusk, and night viewing, and the changes among the palettes are similar for both types of charts. What is unique to the ENC is a broad array of display options that affect how the chart appears on the screen. Many of these are user controlled, others occur automatically in various display configurations. These display variations are outlined here, with reference to subsequent sections for details on the more consequential options.

To accommodate these options, ECS programs implement some form of the ECDIS requirement of having a *Standard display mode* that can be considered the default (or minimum) combination of settings intended as the starting point for chart viewing. Added to that is a *Base display mode* that turns off many of the Standard options for a truly basic view of the chart, which is usually not adequate on its own for general navigation. In the other direction is the *Custom display mode*, sometimes called *Other* or *All*, which turns on (or gives access to) all of the displayable objects within the ENC. The full Custom display is also not often the best choice for general navigation as the chart will be too cluttered. Figure 2.2 -1 shows samples of these three modes.

The intention of the design is the user starts with one of these modes and then turns objects on or off to create a chart display that best meets the needs at hand. This can be a dynamic process, in that you might change the display as you meet changing conditions—or you might find a combination of settings that meet your needs most of the time and then rarely need to change this.

Besides selecting the underlying display mode from the three choices—which is equivalent to selecting a specific subset of objects from the display All option—you can do further quick display adjustments with several toggle (on/off) controls. This toggle option for specific controls is an ECDIS requirement that is met on varying levels by all ECS. For example, regardless of the choice Base, Standard, or All, you can with one click turn soundings on or off; hide text information in several categories; and hide or show various boundaries, light labels, and buoy labels. There is also usually an option to turn on enhanced sector light displays discussed in Section 2.9. The choices offered (and how they are described and implemented) depend on the ECS manufacturer.

Two additional display controls are also available in all ECS programs, namely the option of showing boundary lines as plain lines or symbolized in a way that indicates the meaning of the lines—albeit using a complex coding system—and there is an even more notable option mentioned earlier of using *simplified symbols* versus *paper chart symbols*. Choosing plain boundaries cleans up the chart view notably, but a change of symbols style can be a more significant change to many users. Chapter 4 shows how each of the symbols appear in each style. Examples are also in Section 2.9 on Lights.

The appearance of the water colors and selection of defined depth contours can also be changed by the user in consequential ways. These are covered in Section 2.4. The choice of these depth settings also changes how hazard symbols (rocks, wrecks, obstructions) appear, depending on their individual soundings. Their standard symbols will be automatically replaced with an *isolated danger symbol* whenever their soundings are shallower than the user selected safety depth (also covered in Section 2.4).

There is another unique aspect of ENC display with no counterpart at all in RNCs, namely many objects on the ENC have a *scale minimum* attribute (SCAMIN) that determines which view scales they will be shown on. This is again motivated to provide users with the cleanest possible chart display consistent with safe navigation. This is an

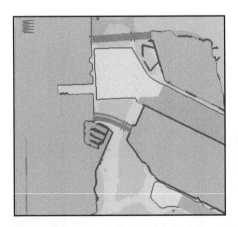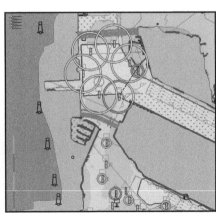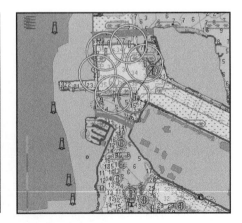

Figure 2.2-1. *Base (left), Standard (center), and All (right) display modes as presented in one particular ECS.*

Table 2.2-1. ENC Display Variations
User Controlled
• **Underlying configuration**
Base, Standard, or All
• **Depth contours and colors**
Shallow, Safety, and Deep
Two colors or four colors
• **Boundary lines**
Plain or Symbolized
• **Symbols style**
Simplified or Paper Chart
• **Toggle on/off**
Soundings
Chart text (several categories)
Light and buoy labels
Enhanced sector-light display
Cable areas
Plus others... (ECS dependent)
Automated changes
• **Active chart in view**
Depends on scale and ECS policy
• **Hiding of symbols**
Depends on scale and ENC specs
• **Isolated danger symbols**
Depends on user-set Safety Contour

automatic change in the display; the attribute is built into the ENC. The end effect is when you zoom out on a region, some objects will disappear. This feature is discussed in Section 2.3.

Table 2.2-1 summarizes the principle ways a user can change the appearance of the chart, plus automated changes the user does not control. The active chart issue included there is discussed in Section 2.3.

Although not related to the charts themselves, there is a significant user interface choice presented by many ECS programs when they implement some form of the ECDIS requirement of providing both a *navigation mode* versus a *planning mode* in the user interface to the chart display. The goal is to have a navigation mode that is restricted to the simplest possible display for safe navigation, usually forced to full-screen display. Thus, route planning or a

study of various derived navigation parameters would be done in the planning mode, which allows about any screen configuration the navigator might choose, in contrast to the navigation mode that is restricted to a simple display that should be less confusing when navigating—usually with larger digits for the numerical data that can be seen some distance away from the screen.

Again, this ECS program interface choice does not affect the chart display itself, and typically the user can switch back to the planning mode for actual navigation if the "navigation mode" does not meet their needs. Screen configurations and typical digital display options for navigation are discussed in Chapter 3.

2.3 Chart Scales

Categories of ENC chart scales (usage bands) were discussed in Section 1.6, and unlike paper charts or RNCs, we know the scale range of an ENC from the name of the chart cell, which is indeed helpful. The physical interpretation of chart scale on paper charts is easy to understand, in that a scale of 1:40,000 means 1 inch on the chart is the same as 40,000 inches on the land or water charted.

This is a more nuanced concept when it comes to electronic charts (RNC or ENC) where we can change the scale with zoom tools. There is no longer an invariant proportion that describes the chart we are looking at. One inch on the screen could be 100 yards or 10 miles, depending on the zoom level of the chart. Thus we end up with two scales to keep in mind: one, the native scale of the electronic chart (called its *compilation scale*), and two, the *view scale* we have selected at the moment.

All ECS programs display the present view scale that applies to the full screen, which could be composed of just one ENC cell or several. If the full screen is just one cell, we can think of a "zoom factor" in the usual way. A chart with compilation scale of 1:20,000 viewed at a scale of 1:10,000 would be a zoom factor of x2.0; viewed at 1:40,000, it would be x0.5—we can never avoid the confusion that small scales are large numbers, because they are thought of as fractions!

The view scale can almost always be changed with plus or minus keys, but how that works depends on the ECS. Some have a fixed list of scale options and the keys go up and down that list. In others, the keys are a fixed zoom step, such as x2.0 per key stroke; in some ECS, adding a second key reduces the size of the steps, offering an almost continuous variation of view scales. Those with a fixed list of scale options often have a drop down menu to go to specific scales. Scale display and its control varies notably from one ECS to the next.

A good way to study your own system is to turn off chart quilting and turn on chart outlines, so you can home in one specific chart at a time, to practice changing zoom levels while maintaining control over the chart and its compilation scale. (Later you will want to turn the quilting back on to see how this complicates the issue!)

It also helps to view an on-screen distance-scale legend as you practice with zoom levels. The ECDIS standard is shown in Figure 2.3-1, but many ECS use their own designs.

The compilation scale of an ENC is usually the same as the corresponding RNC or slightly larger, which is the scale intended for navigation and for a reasonable representation of the precision of the survey in view. This is also the x1.0 view basis for zoomed views.

Overscale (over-zoomed)

For both RNCs and ENCs, a zoomed view of the chart is often helpful and used routinely. The main caution that comes into play with ENC is that the more they are zoomed, the cleaner the display becomes. The cleaner, sharper display of a zoomed ENC, along with its maintaining the same symbol and text sizes, can mislead us into thinking the survey data are as precise as they appear, which might not be the case. The opposite is true with largely over-zoomed RNC, which become pixelated and not reassuring at all.

Indeed, we can over-zoom an ENC to the point where our own GPS position is notably more accurate than the very precise-looking locations of objects in view. Most ECS programs warn the mariner that the view is "over-zoomed" or "overscale" when this potential of misinterpretation is present. A zoom level of > x2 to x4 will trigger this warning, depending on the ECS, but we can use lower zoom levels (i.e. x1.5) without seeing the warning. ECS programs with fixed scale choices only may not allow for an over-zoomed view, which can limit practical navigation. We must be cautious using ECS that do not show an overscale warn-

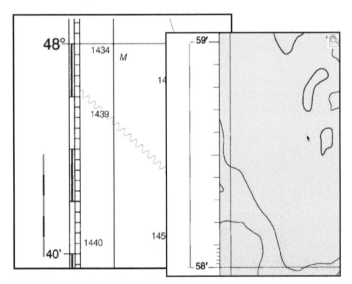

Figure 2.3-1. *ECDIS distance scale legends. The black and gray scale spans a constant 10 nmi; the orange and gray scale spans 1 nmi. The charts shown are not-quilted RNCs, which exposes their borders.*

ing, or have the option to shut it off. The ECDIS standard for over-zoomed warning is x2 (the conservative end), and we can demonstrate cases where x4 leads to disruptive displays that are clearly outside of the chart accuracy. Nevertheless, we can, *with continual awareness of the accuracy limits*, often benefit from a chart view that is over-zoomed. Examples of over-zoomed displays in light of survey accuracy are given in Appendix 1.

We must also keep in mind with regard to overscale warnings, and to scale interpretation generally, that often we view sections of more than one ENC cell at a time on the screen (unless we have turned off the quilting option), and these cells can have different compilation scales. Thus if the left half of the screen is 1:25,000 and the right half is 1:10,000, this view of the full screen could be labeled over-zoomed at a 1:10,000 viewing scale, even though that is the compilation scale of half of the screen. That is, if the ECS in use decided that x2.5 was enough to trigger the overscale warning, it was just the left-hand side accounting for the warning. If we panned the picture to the right without changing the zoom level, so we see only that chart, then the over-zoomed warning will go away. It seems that most ECS programs trigger the warning on the basis of the largest compilation scale in view.

Scaling of ENC can be complex behind the scenes, but outside of the few exceptions we discuss shortly, it is not often a practical issue once you become familiar with your own program's chart display policies. Also, it is often valuable to display two chart windows, one showing a smaller scale for overall perspective on location and the other a larger view for immediate navigation. This procedure is then another way to address over scaling in a single chart window.

Type-approved ECDIS has an option to mark with vertical lines those cells in view that are over-zoomed, but we have not seen this implemented in any ECS we have used. There is a clear risk of this ECDIS feature confusing the display more than helping, which is possibly why ECS programs that are not forced to use it choose not to.

Computer screen resolution

Despite the variability we experience viewing charts on computer screens that can have different screen resolutions and pixel densities, there remains some modicum of the paper chart scale concept. Namely, a line segment on a 1:25,000 chart that is 1 nautical mile long should be (1852 m/25,000) = 7.4 cm (2.9 inches) long when viewed on a paper chart or on a x1.0 display on a computer screen—at least that is an analogy we might pursue.

As an example, using a (1920 x 1076) resolution on a 23.5-inch-wide monitor, which therefore has a pixel density of 82 pixels per inch (ppi), we would expect a one mile line to be about 238 pixels long (82 x 2.9). It is no surprise, however, that various ECS programs do not all present the same video scaling for what they call x1.0. With different

ECS we see a range for the "x1.0" size from what we expected to rather more than expected, namely: 240 (x1.0), 277 (x1.2), 289 (x1.2), and one outlier at 415 (x1.7).

In these latter examples, the "x1.0" image on the screen is magnified somewhat relative to a paper chart expectation. On the other hand, viewing the same chart in the same test programs in a laptop with a 13-inch-wide display at (1440 x 900) resolution with equivalent pixel density of 111 ppi, the same pixel widths translate into x0.7, x0.9, x0.9, and x1.3, which except for the outlier are slight reductions. In short, even though an ECS reports x1.0 on the screen it might not match the paper chart concept of scale for a particular ECS. Nevertheless, the views will all indeed scale as the ECS reports, based on the x1.0 size it shows.

In principle, the ECS could read the screen resolution in use and make adjustments accordingly to the display and overscale (over-zoomed) warnings, but the paper-chart scale analogy remains only a conceptual reference to what we might expect; it is not part of any standard. In electronic charting, the x1.0 (or 100%) display is meant to indicate the normal scale intended for navigation. We may benefit by knowing this is not universal among ECS programs, and that ECS programs designed for tablet devices are aware of the typical screens that will be used, and what constitutes best view for navigation.

Overscale warnings with RNC could be a challenge when using very high resolution displays. On a high resolution tablet or large phone, a measured line segment shows up anywhere between about right (±20%) and three times longer than the same line on the same paper chart beside it, with both displays describing their images as the x1 or 100% view. In short different programs have made different choices here.

Although display variability is notably different between RNC and ENC, both are still in good stead for electronic chart navigation. ENC are much less susceptible to visual changes with scale. An ENC, for example, must meet the symbol size requirements of S-52, which are specified for a pixel density of about 85 ppi, with a minimum screen size of about 11 x 11 inches (270 mm). So once the symbols are drawn the right size, the rest of the chart is composed of just lines (with specified pixel thickness) connecting points, so the views will always look sharp.

Viewing an RNC, we might be puzzled by the size of an object in a x1.0 or 100% view, based on some expectations from paper chart experience, but beyond that we are likely to be very pleased with what we have to work with compared to using the static view of a paper chart—which can depend on having the right pair of glasses at hand in the right level of lighting. It is even common good practice to use a magnifying glass to scan a near shore route on a paper chart to check for hazards. These historic paper chart viewing challenges are a thing of the past with RNC.

NOAA RNC are distributed at a resolution of 400 dpi, so they can be zoomed a factor of 3 or more and still look very sharp. As a rough guideline, an image of 300 dpi is typically considered print quality. However, since both ENC and RNC can look very good when zoomed, we need to keep in mind the accuracy limits of zoomed charts for *both* ENC and RNC.

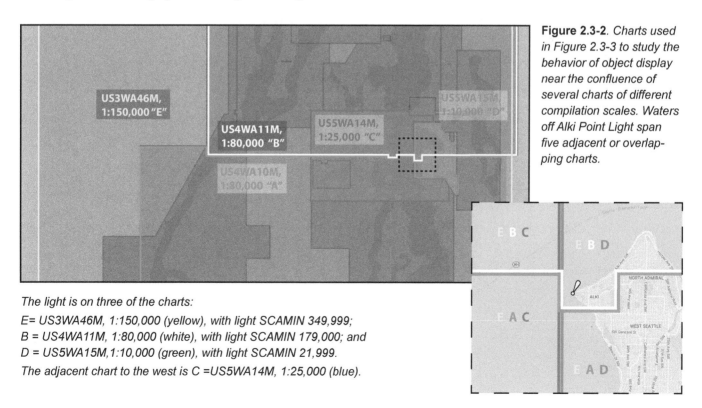

Figure 2.3-2. *Charts used in Figure 2.3-3 to study the behavior of object display near the confluence of several charts of different compilation scales. Waters off Alki Point Light span five adjacent or overlapping charts.*

The light is on three of the charts:
E= US3WA46M, 1:150,000 (yellow), with light SCAMIN 349,999;
B = US4WA11M, 1:80,000 (white), with light SCAMIN 179,000; and
D = US5WA15M,1:10,000 (green), with light SCAMIN 21,999.
The adjacent chart to the west is C =US5WA14M, 1:25,000 (blue).

Minimum scale view of objects

Beyond visual display scale variations we might detect from one ECS program to another, there is a more fundamental aspect to the choice of scale when viewing ENCs. Namely, to meet the IHO goal of presenting the cleanest possible chart view by showing only crucial information, many objects in an ENC have an attribute called *scale minimum* (SCAMIN), which is the minimum viewing scale that the object should appear on. Thus a buoy on a 1:10,000 ENC with SCAMIN of 21,000 (meaning 1:21,000) would show on a view scale of 1:20,000 (or larger) but not on one set to 1:25,000 (or smaller). That functionality can work as intended on some charts in some ECS programs, but in other combinations it can lead to confusion. Furthermore, not all hydrographic offices globally use the scale minimum attribute in their ENCs, and not all ECS programs implement it.

Even restricting the discussion to NOAA ENCs, which do use the SCAMIN attribute, various ECS programs implement it in different ways. Some hide the object at scales smaller than the SCAMIN value (i.e., the object remains in view over a broader range of scales), and other implementations depend on the range of compilation scales in view. Thus you might see a different behavior with quilted charts compared to viewing single charts only. Still other programs implement it in some form, but do not list this attribute in the cursor pick of the objects affected.

An example of SCAMIN in action is shown in Figures 2.3-2 and 2.3-3. These display a common effect of the SCAMIN attribute when applied to depth contour objects, and illustrates the interplay between view scales available to the user and the compilation scales of the charts that cover the region of interest. When two charts of different compilation scales overlap, the ECS has to decide which one to show at various user selected view scales. This is

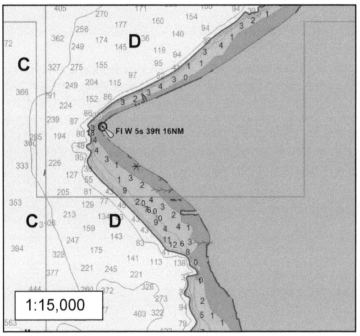

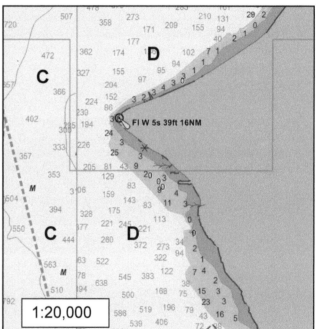

Figure 2.3-3a. *This view at 1:15,000 is a x1.5 view of chart D and a x0.6 view of chart C. Charts shown are identified in Table 2.3-1, which also lists the SCAMIN values that affect what we see. The red lines are chart borders. Since 1:15,000 is larger than both 1:21,999 (the light) and 1:17,999 (depth contours) we see both on chart D, and the contours smoothly match those of chart C.*

Figure 2.3-3b. *When zoomed out to 1:20,000, the viewing scale is now smaller than the SCAMIN attribute value of the contours (17,999) on chart D, so we lose view of them, but this scale is still larger than the SCAMIN of the light (21,999) so the light remains in view. When this happens, the contours abruptly end at the chart boundaries. The density of the soundings in D has gone down slightly (though obscured by the reduced view); the true density included in the chart is only shown when viewed at its compilation scale or larger, 1:10,000 for chart D. Note that although the contour lines were hidden, the user defined depth areas in color remain in view, which are still, for all practical purposes, showing those specific contours.*

Table 2.3-1 Charts shown in Figure 2.3-4				
Chart ID	Chart Name	Chart Scale	SCAMIN	
			Contours	Light
A	US4WA10M	80,000	259,999	—
B	US4WA11M	80,000	259,999	179,000
C	US4WA14M	25,000	44,999	—
D	US5WA15M	10,000	17,999	21,999

a common issue at the boundary between a harbor chart and an approach chart. In the example at hand, we have a 1:10,000 chart (chart D) overlapping a 1:80,000 chart (chart B), and the program has to decide at which view scale it changes the chart?

Suppose this takes place in a particular ECS when the view scale crosses 1:45,000. Then, when viewing at 1:40,000, the program shows us chart D, and viewing at 1:50,000 it shows us chart B. Oftentimes, the user might not even know that the chart in view has changed. At 1:40,000 we are looking at a zoomed-out (x0.25) view of chart D and at 1:50,000 we are looking at a zoomed-in (x1.6) view of chart B. If there happened to be a section of a 1:25,000 chart on the screen at the same time, it would be displayed as x0.5 in this viewer selected 1:50,000 display.

All charts in view are rendered in the viewer selected scale, and when overlapped they will switch back and forth as the user changes view scales to provide the best display within the confines of that particular ECS. What you see depends on the scale options the ECS offers and the algorithm it uses to make the switch. We have in house six high-quality ECS programs we use routinely, and each make these transitions differently. Even the 30 or so type-approved ECDIS programs have large variations on how this important process is rendered. There are simply too many charting configurations possible to make a single rule that will work best in all of them. It is a compromise that each ECS designer must face.

As stated earlier, in many cases you may not detect this switch in charts with scale change, but at the moment we are looking at scenarios where the switch does indeed affect what we see on the chart. Different compilation scales in view at the same time might not be apparent unless we turn on chart outlines and cursor pick each chart to identify the cell—or we might note it by seeing adjacent chart re-

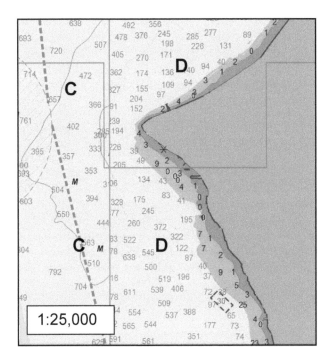

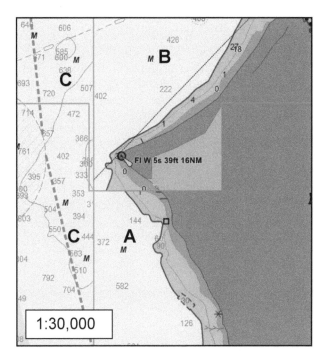

Figure 2.3-3c. *When zoomed out to 1:25,000, the viewing scale is now smaller than the SCAMIN of the light (21,999) on chart D, so we lose view at this particular scale of a major lighthouse on the waterway. Since the compilation scale of the adjacent chart is indeed 1:25,000, this might be an example of a SCAMIN value for this light in the ENC that is not optimal. Again, although we do not see all the contours contained in the ENC of chart D in the last two zoom levels, we still see the colored safety depth areas that are user defined—when set properly, they are usually more important than individual contours.*

Figure 2.3-3d. *When zoomed further out to 1:30,000, which is a x0.33 view of this chart, the ECS decides that this is too far out and switches to the next chart down the stack, which is (somewhat anomalously) a big step down to 1:80,000, chart B for the north part and chart A for the south part. On chart B the SCAMIN of the light is 179,000, so this light is back in view. Now we are at a x2.7 view of this chart, which this ECS evaluates as over-zoomed, so we got a warning (not shown) on the screen, as expected, but not too helpful in this case. The next step out and the warning was removed. Note that in our example in the text, this area switched from chart D to B at 1:45,000 (as some ECS programs do), but the example in the figure switched earlier. In ECS programs that allow only 1:25,000 and 1:50,000 scales, this light is missing on two major scale views.*

gions with different densities of soundings; or we see a set of depth contours abruptly end along a straight line; or we see lights or buoys appear and disappear when we change scales, all of which is, more or less, the subject at hand.

Several examples of this discussion are shown in the panels of Figure 2.3. The key take away point to ENC chart reading in this regard is to understand and anticipate that an active chart in view can change with your view scale selection, and that the attribute SCAMIN can turn objects on and off depending the view scale—and that it can behave differently if you move to a vessel with a different ECS.

Good chart reading practice calls for viewing all charts you plan to use along a route, with the added task with ENCs of zooming in and out along the route to see if this feature might affect your navigation. For example, you might be using a smaller scale chart view for a longer run and then see a light or buoy on the horizon that does not appear on the chart. A logical step then would be to zoom in to see if it shows up.

The affect of the SCAMIN attribute on what you see depends on the scale options offered by your ECS, which vary quite a bit from one brand to the next. Some offer essentially continuous zooming, in both large steps and small; others have a fixed list of scale options; and some of the fixed lists have finer steps than others.

Remember that an ECS display of the present view scale (such as 1:40,000) applies to the full screen of all charts in view—they are all rendered to match that scale—but a screen note such as "x2.5" has to apply to a specific chart on the screen. When these scale factors are employed, which are often useful, we need to learn how to identify which chart on the screen they refer to.

2.4 Soundings, Depth Areas, and Contours

In traditional navigation training we push the topic of water depth to the front of the course, because there is nothing more fundamental to a vessel. Chart scales are a secondary factor with paper charts, in the sense that we have no control over them and we are, after all, looking at the charts when we buy them, and they never change. As shown earlier, however, chart scales play a more crucial role with ENC use, so we just now get to the water itself.

Soundings retain their same meaning in ENC, i.e., they are not just water depths, they are water depths that have actually been measured—it could have been a long time ago, but they were measured. This accounts for some charts having more soundings than others, because they are charts with better hydrographic surveys. The first key point is, soundings on an ENC are one-to-one the same as those on the RNC it was based upon—but we do have new soundings-related options in the ENC.

Using ENCs, we are no longer restricted to the sounding units on the paper chart or RNC, which is an issue primarily for the use of NOAA charts, since most nations use meters to begin with. The inherent units of all ENC are meters, but this is easily changed in any ECS to display feet or fathoms if desired.

ENC soundings also have the same reference level as on RNCs; they are measured from the depth of the water when the tide is zero. Technically, the soundings are indeed ENC objects (SOUNDG) with attributes (discussed further at the end of this section), but we have not seen an ECS offer cursor pick information, unless (rarely) they are circled, meaning they are uncertain. A line of constant sounding is a depth contour, and the contours can be clicked to confirm their sounding value. On the other hand, every charted object in the water that can be covered by the tide does have a *value of sounding* attribute (VALSOU). A rock with a sounding value of 2.3 m means, when the tide is zero, the top of the rock is 2.3 m below the surface. Drying heights are presented as negative soundings.

Figure 2.4-1. *Four-color and two-color water displays. The four colors are standardized, but they vary from one ECS to the next, sometimes notably. Also shown are several cursor pick reports from depth areas and contours. The areas can be interrogated anywhere between the contours, but the cursor pick must be precisely on the contour line. The values shown will be the next deepest ones to the numerical values entered. To highlight a specific one, click it to learn its value, then enter one slightly below that. Some ECS can show contour labels; others do not.*

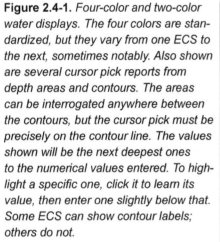
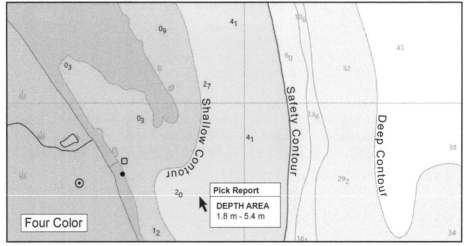

A rock with a sounding value of -1.5 m, means the top of the rock is 1.5 m above the water when the tide is zero. An isolated sounding of 7.3 meters would be displayed as a subscript with the same font size for both digits (7_3).

Safety Depth

Soundings in ENCs are displayed in two different colors, depending on a user selected *safety depth*. Soundings shallower than the safety depth are printed black so they stand out, and soundings deeper than the safety depth are a shade of gray, so they are less distracting. This is a subtle but very practical display feature that becomes more clear after we discuss depth contours.

This safety feature, and other depth related options discussed below, depends on the user entering the proper value of the safety depth for their vessel, taking into account any variations of the tide they might encounter. None of the depth related features of an ECS account for a changing tide—even though most ECS can indeed compute the tide level at the nearest station, as discussed in Section 3.11.

What might not have been suspected, however, is ENCs display the same depth contours as used on their corresponding RNC. We might have guessed that since the ENC knows the location of every sounding, it could in principle create depth contours of its own using some interpolation scheme, but that is not the case. The contours transfer directly from RNC to ENC. Since charts of different scales often have contours at different spacings, we can expect some mismatches at chart boundaries, just as we observe using RNCs.

Depth Area

A valuable new feature of ENC is the object *depth area* (DEPARE), which is an area object defined by two adjacent depth contours. The value it reports when cursor picking any point on the water is the range defined by the two charted contour depths on either side of the point clicked. Thus a pick report of "depth area: 5.4 m - 9.1 m," means the water depth is somewhere between these two values.

If you click the contour itself on the deep water side, the report would be "depth contour: 9.1 m." Thus we cannot just click the chart and read the water depth, but we do know the range of depths at any point. This cursor pick also confirms the sounding units as they are reported with the depth area

Again, in principle, the ECS could report an interpolated depth at any point just as geographic information system (GIS) programs do for points on land, but for now we get a range, not a specific depth—and it is easy to look at the bathymetry of some waterways to see that this could be risky in cases where it matters. Nevertheless, the depth area report is still a very useful function.

Safety Contour

Depth contours in general play a far more important role in ENCs than we are accustomed to when using RNCs. We are restricted to using the contours native to specific charts, but they play a much more dynamic role in chart usage and safe navigation. All ECS employ the unique IHO concept of a *safety contour*, which affects how the chart looks and how various safety features of the ECS respond. The safety contour is intended to mark the waters that are unsafe for your vessel. They will become a prominent darker blue. The default value is 30 m, but it must be set for individual vessels. There is, however, a special relationship between the safety depth and the safety contour that is crucial to understand.

We are challenged in this relationship because of the varied ways these values are entered into an ECS. Most ECS offer the inputs for three depths related to safe navigation and chart display: Shallow, Safety, and Deep. These are sometimes labeled "depths" and sometimes "contours," and frankly it would be difficult to say which is best, as we shall see. The one marked safety is the crucial one. The other two (deep and shallow) are only there because the IHO standard is to offer either a two-color or a four-color depth display pattern. The values of deep and shallow water affect the colors of the water in a four-color display, as shown in Figure 2.4-1, but nothing else. They do not make any difference at all to the display or function of your chart when you choose a two-color display. The deep and shallow water inputs apply to the four-color display only.

With all three depth inputs, we must remember that the ECS can only display contours that are built into the ENC, so if we choose our deep water as 20 m, but there is no 20 m contour, it will initiate the deep water color at the next deepest contour contained in the chart, which could be 90 m. This will start the deep water color at 90 m on the

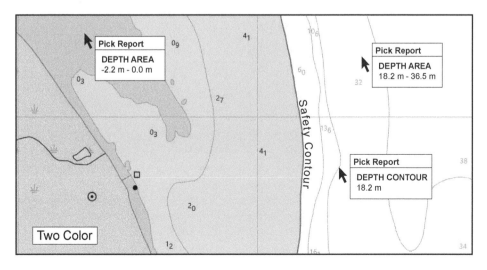

display, but your deep water input field will maintain the input value of 20 m. Likewise, your choice of shallow water will be bounced to the next deepest contour, but retain the number you typed in.

Now the distinctions begin between the behavior of the deep and shallow inputs, and the important one labeled "safety." The numbers you see in the deep and shallow fields are only used to find the next deepest contours in order to paint the water colors; the actual values you chose and see listed in the input fields have no other significance. This is not the case with the safety input of a typical ECS.

The IHO standard has two concepts with similar names: *safety depth* and *safety contour*. These are not the same, but most ECS programs use the same input for both parameters—hence our ambiguity in what is the best label for this input. The numerical value you type into the "safety depth" / "safety contour" field is your chosen safety depth, regardless of its label. That value determines the colors of the soundings, black or gray, as discussed earlier. The safety depth in turn is what is used to find the next deepest contour on the chart to mark as your safety contour. That contour will show up as bold so that it stands out from all of the others. The location of that important contour affects appearance of isolated danger symbols, as well as triggering various look-ahead safety alarms.

The safety contour will be bold and prominent on both two-color displays (one color on either side of it) and on four-color displays (two colors on either side of it.) But more importantly, the number that remains showing in the input field now has a physical meaning that affects the chart view. This is important to note, because often the safety contour can be significantly deeper than your chosen safety depth, as it can only be selected from the pre-determined contours. If the input field in your particular ECS happens to be labeled "safety depth" then that will be the reminder of what it is; if that field is labeled "safety contour," then we have to remember what more it means.

The two-color display is the default setting in most programs and likely the easiest display to interpret. Since the standard colors do vary from one ECS to the next, practice with the layouts is crucial for the four-color option.

Units

In 1991, Executive Order 12770 instructed the Department of Commerce, which oversees NOAA, to finally implement Metric Conversion Act of 1975 and called for prompt transition to the metric scale. To NOAA's credit, they did indeed then begin to print nautical charts with meters on the back of the traditional feet or fathoms charts, which was especially useful for U.S. waters bordering Canada. But as several years went by, short of a few metric unit equivalents in parenthesis, no other agencies made any of the difficult choices NOAA/OCS had made—and no one complained. Consequently, NOAA discontinued this added expense in about 1997 and returned to feet or fathoms only.

There were no legal issues and no discussion in the news about this, because, sure enough, Section 2 (a) (1) of the same Executive Order stated "Metric usage shall not be required to the extent that such use is impractical or is likely to cause significant inefficiencies or loss of markets to United States firms."

With that background, we can appreciate that the mandated use of ENCs in U.S. commercial shipping as well as its increasing popularity amongst all mariners, is our first real step toward making this important transition. The base units for heights and depths in all ENC are meters, and even though we can change the units displayed in our ECS, meters are now an inescapable part of our maritime life.

But we do not escape the remnants of the mixed units when using NOAA ENCs. These charts are rendered from

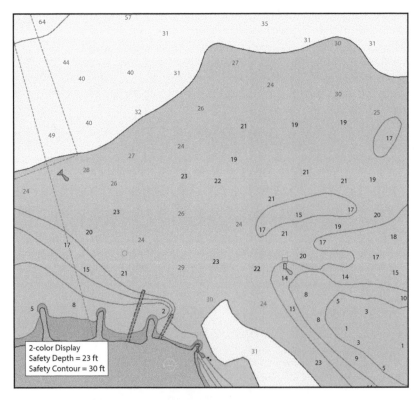

Figure 2.4-2. *Safety depth and safety contour in action. The choice of a safety depth of 23 ft defines the next deepest contour (30 ft) as the safety contour, and makes it bold with a prominent color change. The value of 23 ft also instructed the ECS to make all soundings shallower than 23 ft black, so they stand out from other soundings. Thus we see from the soundings color, that our safe water extends somewhat into the blue, where soundings are gray, and there is indeed a safe passage into the channel. Recall, we must take tide variation into account on selecting the safety depth for our vessel.*

Table 2.4-1 Rounding of Soundings*				
	A	B	C	D
RNC fm	RNC ft	ENC m	ECS ft	ECS fm
1	6	1.8	5.9	1.0
2	12	3.6	11.8	2.0
3	18	5.4	17.7	3.0
5	30	9.1	29.9	5.0
10	60	18.2	59.7	10.0
20	120	36.5	119.8	20.0
100	600	182.8	599.7	100.0

* A marks typical contours in ft; B is how they appear in an ENC; C is how the ECS program reports them back in feet units. D shows there is no such issue with fathom units.

RNCs that use feet. Thus you see in a meters display, shallow contours labeled 3_6, 5_4, and 18_2, meaning 3.6 m, etc. This is not a surprise, because they represent contours at 12, 18, and 60 feet that end up with these decimal values when converted to meters, taking into account the IHO standard of using 0.1 m precision.

What could be a surprise, and the point that we are getting to, is when you display these same contours in a feet display, they will be shown by cursor pick to be 11.8 ft, 17.7 ft, and 59.7 ft and not the 12.0, 18.0 and 60.0 ft we know they are. Recalling that the definition of the inch as exactly 2.54 cm is what links the English and Metric systems, the exact conversion is 1 m = (100/2.54/12) ft. The ECS does this properly, converting the precise meter values in the ENC back to feet, but NOAA had to make a compromise with their original conversion of feet to meters. To provide the mandated tenth-meter precision they could have rounded the exact conversion to tenths, but what they actually do is simply truncate all digits beyond the tenth-meter position, i.e., for 18 ft (5.4864... m) we get 5.4 m rather than 5.5 m.

If you round, rather than truncate, you get reconverted feet contours (column C in Table 2.4-1) that are half above the base values (column A) and half below, but when you truncate you are guaranteed that the reconverted feet values are all just below the base values, which is a consistent result. Also by truncating, all contours plotted are guaranteed to be deeper (by a few inches) than labeled, never shallower, which is philosophically a better choice. This does not apply to contours expressed in fathoms, which reproduce identically, and indeed the 0.3 ft discrepancy we see in feet units is still within the IHO standard precision of 0.1 m.

This does have a minor side implication. If you choose to highlight a specific contour on the chart (feet or meters) for any reason, deep water, shallow, or safety, then we would typically enter a value just less than its charted value, and the program would find the next one up that we wanted. But if you wanted, for example, to highlight 18 ft,

you could not enter 17.7 or higher, as it would move to the next one out. For this operation it is safest to cursor pick the contour you want to highlight, and then enter something just less than that.

There are not many reasons to select a contour that way, because usually it is the vessel draft and tides that determine the choice, at least for the safety contour. But there are cases where local knowledge or traditional routes call for following a specific contour and if that one is on the

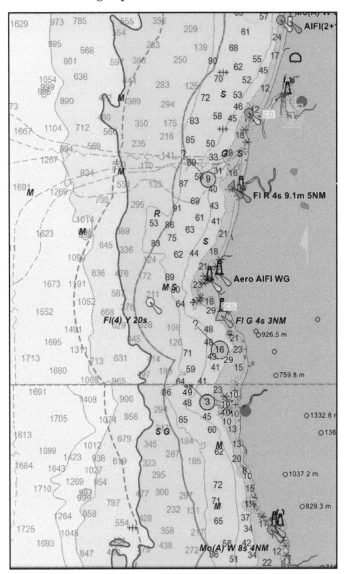

Figure 2.4-3. *Using the contour assignments in an ENC for open-ocean routing relative to the location of the continental shelf. In certain wind and sea conditions, the sea state along the edge of the shelf can be notably steeper than well off to either side of it. It is good practice for smaller vessels transiting the coast to keep in mind the location of this shelf, which typically drops off at about 100 fathoms. In this example, contours are selected at the edge of the shelf (100 fm) and at the ocean surface (1000 fm). The shallow water contour was set at 20 fm. When traveling in closer to shore, a new set of contours would be selected in the normal manner related to safe depths and other concerns.*

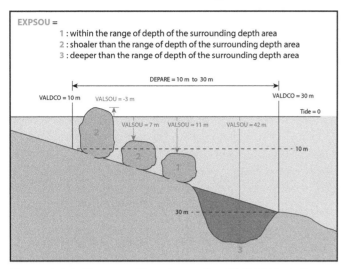

Figure 2.4-4. *The exposition of sounding (EXPSOU) attribute of a sounding specifies its value relative to the depth area that includes it.*

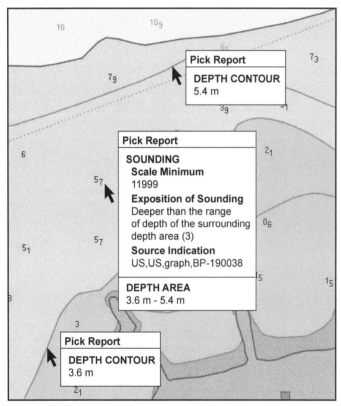

Figure 2.4-5. *Exposition of Sounding attribute used to emphasize that a sounding is outside the depth area range. Source indication for this sounding references a specific hydrographic survey. In future ENCs we might learn the specific numerical uncertainty in this sounding via a Zone of Confidence report. In contrast to ECDIS, not all ECS offer cursor picks of individual soundings.*

chart, this is one way to mark it. This is the ENC equivalent of using a highlight pen to mark a contour of interest on a paper chart.

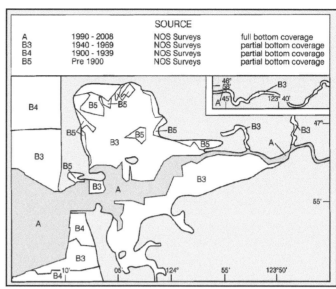

Figure 2.4-6. *Source diagram from chart 18502, which outlines general quality sounding data. B4 and B5 indicates lead line and sextant measurements, with likelihood of missed features. Region A indicates data acquired by side scan sonar or multibeam sonar technology using differential GPS positioning. Undetected features in this area, at the time of the survey, would be unlikely. B3 data were acquired by continuous recording single beam echo sounder. It is possible that features could have been missed between the sounding lines, although echo sounders record all depths along a sounding line with varying beam widths. Other source categories are defined in the U.S. Coast Pilot.*

Another example of this selective contour highlighting is the route along the West Coast, where we want to avoid the edge of the continental shelf, sailing either well inside it or outside of it. The seas along the shelf in some conditions can be markedly more severe than away from it. We can mark the edge of the continental shelf at about 100 fathoms and ocean beyond it at about 1000 fathoms, as shown in Figure 2.4-3. The area near the "safety contour" is what we want to avoid. We are not using it for grounding or obstruction warnings, we are using it to mark potentially hazardous seas.

Attributes of Soundings

Although not displayed in all ECS programs, the ENC includes attributes of soundings that could be crucial to a depth related routing decision. For one, they have a *scale minimum* (SCAMIN) that accounts for why they are not seen at certain zoom levels, and when the sounding is not consistent with the depth area they will report an *exposition of sounding* (EXPSOU), which is defined in Figure 2.4-4. This attribute can be applied to individual soundings or to objects that cover and uncover. When applied to a sounding, it seems to imply there is an incomplete survey in the region, otherwise there would be another contour present, as shown in Figure 2.4-5.

Another promising potential for the use of ENC going forward is the *source indication* (SORIND) attribute as

ZOC CATEGORIES (Refer to Chapter 1, United States Coast Pilot)				
ZOC	DATE	POSITION ACCURACY	DEPTH ACCURACY	SEAFLOOR COVERAGE
A1	2008	± 16 ft	= 1.6 ft + 1%d	All significant seafloor features detected.
B	1979	± 164 ft	= 3.3 ft + 2%d	Uncharted features hazardous to surface navigation are not expected but may exist.
C	1939	± 1600 ft	= 6.6 ft + 2%d	Depth anomalies may be expected.
D	---	Worse than ZOC C	Worse than ZOC C	Large depth anomalies may be expected.
MD	Maintained Depth - See Chart			

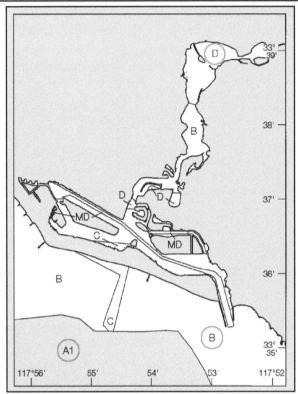

Figure 2.4-7. *Zone of Confidence diagram from paper chart 18754, Newport Beach, CA. This is one of the first charts to replace the traditional Source Diagrams with ZOC data. These data are now incorporated into the corresponding ENC, Figure 2.4-8. The red circles mark the regions of the quality of data reports shown in Figure 2.4-8.*

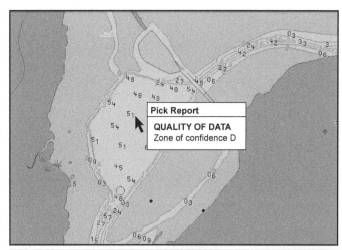

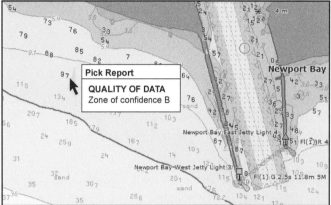

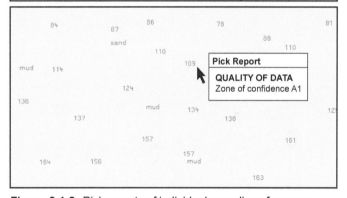

Figure 2.4-8. *Pick reports of individual soundings from sample locations on chart US5CA83M, reflecting the new trend to include specific soundings accuracy in the* quality of data *object report. Accuracies for specific ZOCs are shown in Figure 2.4-7. The full list is in the* U.S. Coast Pilot. *The same information is found under a depth area report. Note that the* quality of data object *is often shut off on displays as default, because it can clutter the screen in other situations.*

applied to soundings. A sample is shown in Figure 2.4-5. Many soundings on this ENC show their source as just the RNC chart number it was based upon, but in other parts of the chart we get references to specific hydrographic surveys (i.e., BP-190038), which are actually online with numeric uncertainties listed. Unfortunately, the SORIND attribute is often not displayed, and even when it is, the data presented in it is just a first step in the documentation of sounding accuracy that can be included in an ENC. There is in certain cases, however, even more detailed data accuracy information available that can have an impact on navigation.

Precise, documented soundings along with new technologies such as NOAA's Air Gap program for measuring bridge clearances, in real time, to within inches, allows draft limits in harbors to be set more precisely, opening up new shipping options for the region. Accurate soundings also affect shallow water navigation and shoreline construction projects.

A new major change in the presentation of chart accuracy data has been initiated on paper charts as well. The new method is explained in Chapter 1 of every *U.S. Coast*

Pilot, but so far, very few of the 1000+ NOAA charts are employing it. The (soundings) Source Diagrams we are accustomed to seeing on paper charts (Figure 2.4-6) are being replaced by Zones of Confidence (ZOC) diagrams (Figure 2.4-7) that are very specific about the uncertainties for both positional and vertical accuracy of the soundings. Data from these ZOC diagrams are encoded in an ENC as the attribute *category of zone of confidence* (CATZOC) of the object *quality of data* (M_QUAL). An example is shown in Figure 2.4-8. Again, there are only a few NOAA charts (RNC and ENC) that include this sophisticated specification of the accuracy, but it is a fine example of the enhanced utility of the ENCs of the future.

The ZOC data when available can be used to numerically investigate the concepts of over-zooming in relation to crucial issues of navigation in close proximity to landmarks and near shore depth contours.

2.5 Isolated Danger Symbol

A valuable new concept in the ECDIS standard calls for the display of an *isolated danger symbol* whenever the sounding of a rock, wreck, or obstruction is less than the value of the safety contour—or when its sounding is unknown. Several popular ECS programs implement this function, but not all. The symbol is conspicuous and valuable in many applications. See Figure 2.5-1.

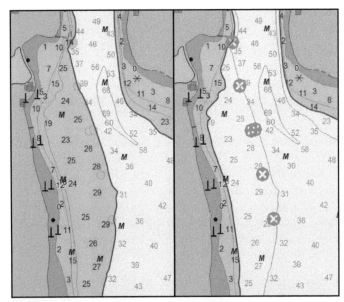

Figure 2.5-1. *Isolated danger symbols triggered here by underwater obstructions (dotted circles) with unknown depths. On the left they are on the unsafe side of the safety contour (29.9 ft) and are not marked; but with safety contour reduced to 17.7 ft, they are then located in "safe" water and marked as isolated dangers. These obstructions are components of an abandoned underwater pipeline, whose depths are not known.*

It is triggered by the safety contour, not the safety depth value, so display could be distracting in some cases, depending on safety contour selection. ECS programs that offer this option, include option to not use it.

2.6 Rocks

Now we come to a topic that may be of more interest to recreational mariners than to professionals because the former spend more time close in along the shoreline where most of the rocks are located. To small-craft mariners under sail, power, or even paddle, the way rocks are charted is crucial to their safe navigation. That is not to say ships don't hit rocks; there are famous cases in the news. The goal of any change in charting must be toward improved safety for all vessels, keeping in mind that most accidents can be traced to operator errors. So if symbol and notation changes are going to be made, we want them to be made in the right direction—toward minimizing errors in chart reading.

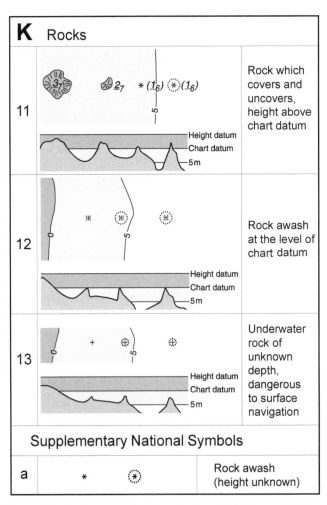

Figure 2.6-1. *Samples of paper chart symbols from U.S. Chart No. 1. Other nations and the IHO do not single out U.S. symbol Ka (isolated asterisk with no label) as a special symbol and instead include it in category K11. See Note on Terminology.*

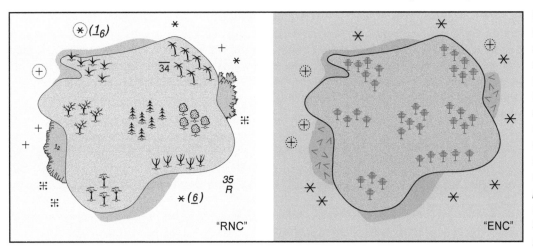

Figure 2.6-2. *Rock and terrain symbols are greatly simplified on ENC charts. Left is a hypothetical RNC (paper chart, INT 1); right is the corresponding ENC. The six or so INT 1 rock symbols used on paper charts are covered in ENC with just two symbols, with detailed attributes found by cursor pick. Likewise the attractive but challenging INT 1 trees notation is replaced with a generic tree and a cursor pick. Using ENCs, navigation schools will have to forgo tricky test questions distinguishing INT 1 coral from rocks, as these two are a single generic symbol on ENC. Click the symbol to find out which. (We leave it as an exercise to decide which is coral and which is rocks in the RNC.)*

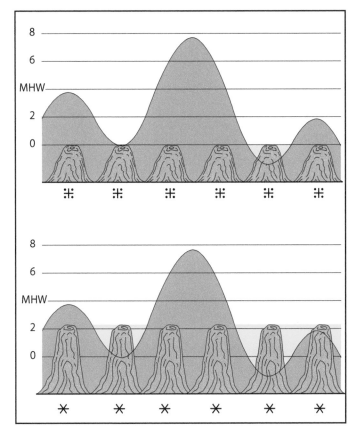

Figure 2.6-3. *An aside to recall why the rock awash had its own symbol in the days of paper charts! Top is a rock awash at chart sounding datum (i.e., tide equals zero), with its corresponding unique paper chart symbol. Bottom is a rock which covers and uncovers; ENCs use the same symbol (an asterisk) for both types of rock. Yellow marks the time span of the tidal cycle during which each is uncovered, to emphasize the greater hazard of the rock with zero or near zero sounding.*

The use and meaning of rock symbols on ENCs are not the same as they are on paper charts. We have gone from seeing some 6 or 7 "rock symbols" that tell us much about the rock from the symbol alone, to seeing just two different rock symbols on an ENC, some of which may not show at all—being replaced by an isolated danger symbol as noted earlier.

Thus we come back to the primary new approach to chart reading when using ENCs; cursor-picking any object we want to know about. This is especially crucial for rocks. ENC rock symbols alone do not convey detailed information.

This change in chart reading practice required when using ENCs can be a challenge, depending on individual experience. Having used paper charts for 30 years, my initial attitude toward these simplifications of the symbols, and rock symbology in particular, was negative, and I was not timid in complaining about it. However, the more I have used ENCs and studied the goals of the IHO in their "new" system (it is actually some 10 years old at this point!), I have changed my opinion on this.

Although we might miss our traditional symbols, there is much virtue in not having to learn all the nuances of the traditional rock symbols in the first place. In fact, many mariners who did not need to know these details to pass a navigation exam may not have been aware of all the information contained in the paper chart symbols. It is not even that transparent when searching *U.S. Chart No. 1*, the official source for paper chart symbols. Part of Section K on rocks is shown in Figure 2.6-1

Note on Terminology
The IHO definition (S-32) of "rock awash" is a rock that is awash at tide height equals zero, whereas the *Bowditch* definition of "rock awash" is a rock that is awash at *any* tide height between zero and MHW. This can be helpful to recall when an ENC pick report describes "Water level affect = awash."

Using ENCs, we only have to teach that there are two types of rock symbols, an isolated asterisk or an isolated plus sign in a dotted circle (Figure 2.6-2). To know more about that rock, just click it. The procedure is easier to learn than memorizing multiple symbols, and probably a safer way to use charts. We must train ourselves to click every rock that is near our route.

On ENCs, an asterisk symbol is a rock that covers and uncovers as the tide changes between zero and the height datum (MHW on U.S. charts). These include paper chart rocks K11, K12, and Ka. The encircled plus sign is a rock that is always covered when the tide is zero, which is paper chart rock K13. Note that we see a plus sign with or without a ring of dots on an RNC, but it aways has a ring of dots on an ENC. A ring of dots in all charting means a special hazard.

When we cursor pick a rock on an ENC, we will be given the depth or drying height as the attribute *value of sounding* (VALSOU). An asterisk rock with a (4) beside it on a Canadian RNC will report a sounding of -4.0 m in the corresponding ENC. In ENC reports, a negative sounding is a drying height.

A drying height is how high a rock is above the water when the tide height is zero. On paper charts, drying heights are marked by an underlined number, say (8), usually in parenthesis so it is not confused with a sounding. On U.S. RNC, this would mean 8 ft, which brings up still another point. This would mean 8 ft on a U.S. RNC, *even if the soundings units on the chart were fathoms.* A definite virtue of the ENC is the base units of the charts are always meters, both for heights and soundings. So this is

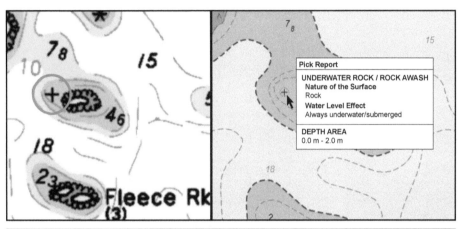

Figure 2.6-4. *Underwater rock on an RNC (left) and an ENC (right). These always have a ring of dots on ENCs, but not necessarily on RNCs.*

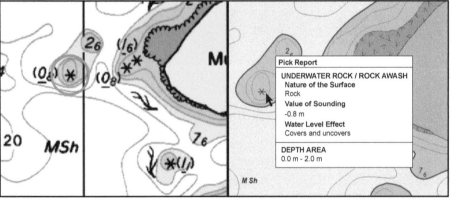

Figure 2.6-5. *Rock that covers and uncovers on an RNC (left) and an ENC (right). The drying height is shown as a negative sounding on an ENC.*

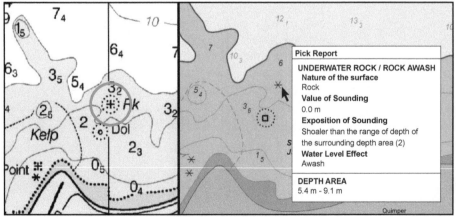

Figure 2.6-6 *Rock awash at tide height zero on an RNC (left) and an ENC (right). This type of rock is called a "rock awash" in IHO terminology, but any rock that covers and uncovers is called "rock awash" in Bowditch terminology. See Note on Terminology.*

another nuance we do not have to face when using ENC. Mariners can choose to change the display units from meters to feet or fathoms, but when doing so, *all* units will be consistent; there will not be soundings in one unit and drying heights in another.

ENC rocks that cover and uncover do not display the drying height next to the symbol, even if it is known. If the drying height is not known, we get in the cursor pick report "Value of sounding unknown."

Then there is the small-craft mariner's rock of horrors, namely one that is just awash at tide height zero. On paper charts this is marked with a + sign with dots in each quadrant (K12)—an appropriately unique rock symbol. This is especially dangerous rock because it is always within the tide range of the surface, but is only exposed during the rare times the tide is negative. See Figure 2.6-3. For small craft navigators, knowing the tide height is crucial when these rocks are near.

This traditional paper chart symbol of a plus sign with four dots is not used in ENC, and so we only identify it by "Value of the sounding = 0.0" on a cursor pick. Several examples of rocks shown on RNCs compared to ENCs are in Figures 2.6-4 to 2.6-6.

In summary, in the ENC rock presentation we lose drying height information from the visual symbol and any special warnings about K12 rocks, but gain a logical reporting system. Since we are now cursor picking every rock near us, when we learn, for example, that a rock has a drying height of 0.2 m (i.e., value of sounding = -0.2 m,) we can appreciate that this is just as dangerous and essentially as unlikely to be visible as one that has drying height of exactly 0.0 that gets a special symbol on paper charts.

Also, the introduction of the isolated danger symbol in the ENCs goes a long way to protecting mariners from hitting covered rocks when they have their safety contour programmed properly in the customized vector chart display settings (Section 2.5).

We obviously rely on the rock's attributes being correct in the ENC and being clearly presented by the ECS. If we observe rocks that are not documented, or incorrectly so, there are convenient ways to report this to the HO respon-

sible (Section 1.3), which can in turn quickly make the updates. A recurring theme of this book is the ENC will just get better with time—with our help.

2.7 Buoys

When learning about buoys on paper charts, we teach the basic symbol conventions and point out that you can usually tell from the chart what a specific buoy is marking or intended to mean. That remains true using ENCs; it is just easier now with the cursor pick reports that categorize the buoys, often with a name that identifies it further, along with other properties that assist mariners with the use of buoys. Knowing color and shape conventions of various buoys is not as crucial with ENC as all that information is provided. Buoy categories are listed in Table 2.7-1.

Each buoy object then has a list of attributes that include: color, color pattern, shape, name, and category that describes its purpose. The system of navigational marks (IALA A or B) is also always included, which can be valuable on the borders between these regions. Beyond these basics, we also might learn special information such as status (seasonal, etc), scale minimum, radar reflector, or even its vertical length (water level to highest point), but we have yet to see this dimension recorded for buoys.

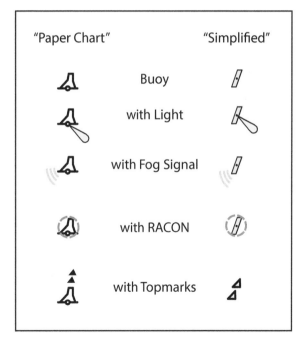

Figure 2.7-1. *Sample buoy symbols, this one of a pillar buoy, showing both display options. An individual buoy symbol can show none or any combination of these extra objects on the buoy. The full list of all buoy symbols is in Chapter 4. The S-52 standard for paper chart buoys is just a black outline as shown, but many ECS present them with their actual colors. Topmarks are most often associated with cardinal buoys, which are not used in the U.S.. We have added extra discussion on these in Chapter 4.*

Table 2.7-1 Buoy Objects	
Type	*Acronym*
Lateral	BOYLAT
Isolated danger	BOYISD
Safe water	BOYSAW
Special purpose	BOYSPP
Cardinal	BOYCAR
Mooring*	MORFAC

* A mooring buoy is considered a category of a mooring facility *object.*

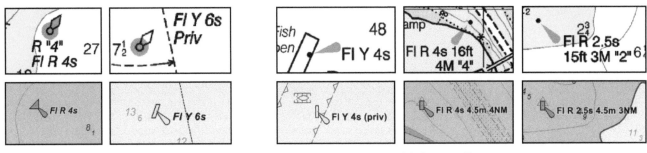

Lighted Buoys   Lights on Beacons

Figure 2.7-2. *Samples of lighted buoys and lights on beacons seen in RNCs and paper charts (top) and on ENCs (bottom). Notice that simplified ENC buoys and beacons are similar symbols, but ENC buoys maintain the paper chart convention of leaning over as if in current along with the text leaning over (italics) as well.*

Buoys can also have lights, topmarks, fog signals, racons, AIS, etc. but within the S-57 standard these are separate objects; they are not attributes of the buoy object. Each of these additional features of the buoy installation change the symbol as shown in Figure 2.7-1, so we can from the symbols alone anticipate they are there, but how we are told the details of each in a pick report depends on the specific ECS program we are using. We find that different ECS use different rules on this. Many, rationally, treat a buoy with a light and fog signal, as related objects, so a single click of the buoy symbol brings up the report for all three.

Other ECS programs completely separate these components of the combined symbol to the extent that we only learn about the light if we specifically click the flare symbol, or about the fog signal by clicking the sound wave part of the symbol. In these cases, clicking the buoy only tells about the buoy itself. We have also seen programs that have these objects separated, with individual reports on each part, but if you click the very center of the symbol common to all components then you get the report on all parts there.

In short, we could hope for more standardization of the ECS cursor pick conventions for buoy symbols, but in all cases, all information is available; these notes just alert users to this variability.

Looking ahead to Section 2.9 on lights and beacons, it could be beneficial to point out a subtle philosophy change in the ENC symbology compared to what we are used to on paper charts. On paper charts, a lighted buoy was indicated by a magenta circle on top of the buoy symbol, and flare symbols, no matter where they appeared on the chart, indicated lights on beacons (fixed to the ground). There was no possible confusion with a light on a beacon and a light on a buoy, as shown in the top of Figure 2.7-2. This seems an improvement, but coming from paper charts it can take a while for this change to settle in. Two

flares beside each other were instinctively considered two fixed lights, but now they can be that, or two buoys, or one of each—a closer look to the symbol resolves this.

2.8 Datums, Horizontal and Vertical

A *datum* is an official reference or standard that is used for measurements. There are four datums that come into play with the use of ENCs, and the commonly-used terminology for these is not as tidy as we might hope. There is one horizontal datum, used for relating the location of a landmark with a latitude and longitude on the chart, and there are three vertical datums, one used for soundings, one for heights, and one for elevations.

The horizontal datum is nicely resolved when using ENCs, as this is always World Geodetic System of 1984

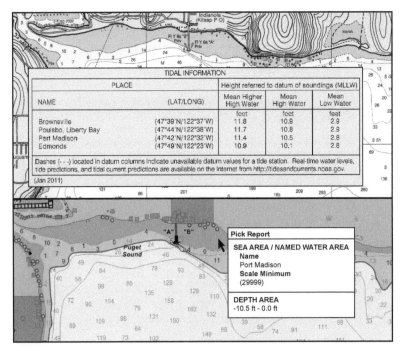

Figure 2.8-1. *An RNC (top) with an insert showing tidal data that is located elsewhere on the chart and moved here for display, and (bottom) an ENC of the same region showing how we can learn the numerical value of the height datum (MHW) from the depth area of the foreshore zone.*

(WGS84). ENCs use WGS84 for all dates and for all locations, globally. Thus, you will want to have your GPS datum selection set to WGS84 when using an ENC. The issues we face using printed charts or RNCs that use other datums do not apply to ENCs. (Note that WGS84 is essentially the same as North American Datum of 1983, so no positioning issues are likely when using an RNC with that horizontal datum.)

Unfortunately, most paper charts simply list the name of this datum prominently under the chart title, without identifying it further, which has led to referring to this datum as "the chart datum." Elsewhere on paper charts, notes refer to this as the "horizontal datum," which is indeed a better reference. For best communications, we want to avoid the generic phrase "chart datum."

The two vertical dimensions we care about on ENCs are heights and depths. The depths (soundings) are easy. For all charts, these are referenced to a water level when the tide is zero. That is the key point we need to know about the sounding datum. It is hard to imagine a case where we would ever care how that datum was established, nor even what tide level it corresponds to. It could be mean lower low water (MLLW) used in the U.S., or lower low water, large tide (LLWLT) used in Canada, or lowest astronomical tide used in the UK. The hydrographic office making the charts are the same ones that choose the datums, and they are the same ones who tell us the tide height. All soundings are referenced to tide height equals zero, and that is all we need to know. Again, unfortunately, this datum is also often referred to as "the chart datum." And again, we should avoid that, and if there ever was any reason to refer to this datum, it would best be called the "sounding datum."

When it comes to interpreting the vertical heights of lights, landmarks, terrain, and bridge clearances, however, the datum issue becomes more nuanced, and for these

we do indeed need to know what vertical datum they refer to, which of course means knowing what it is called, how is it defined, and what the actual value is. This is not as obvious as it might seem.

Our experience with paper charts is the starting point. NOAA paper charts have a prominent statement near the title "Heights in feet above mean high water," which, though not using the terminology, is defining the vertical height datum as mean high water. A light on a U.S. chart listed as 30 ft high means the light is 30 ft above the water surface when the tide height equals mean high water (MHW). All paper charts include a table of the values of MHW for several locations across the chart. A sample is shown in the top of Figure 2.8-1. The vertical datum is MHW and the value of the datum at Brownsville, WA is 10.9 ft. If the tide at the moment happened to be 5.2 ft, which is 5.7 ft below MHW, then this light would be 30 + 5.7 = 35.7 ft above the surface. Likewise, a charted bridge clearance of 50 ft, would have at the moment an extra 5.7 ft of clearance at this tide level, or a total air gap of 55.7 ft.

This datum is sometimes referred to as the "vertical datum," but since we have more than one vertical datum in use on the chart, it would be best to call this simply the "height datum."

Once we move on to ENCs, however, the issue of height datum becomes an immediate challenge. First, there is indeed an attribute assigned to many objects called *vertical datum* (VERDAT), even though we do not see it very often in pick reports. This same attribute, however, can be used for both sounding datum and height datum. The values the cartographer can enter for the attribute VERDAT are essentially any one of the known tide levels, high or low, or it can be populated with choice #24 "Local datum." In either case, the attribute VERDAT is the definition of the datum, and not its actual value; furthermore, as noted, VERDAT itself is rarely seen reported by ECS programs.

The tide level used for the height datum is encoded into every ENC (in meta object M_VDAT), but it is up to the ECS to display it. We are surprised to see that many ECS programs do not present this, although all type-approved ECDIS do. In principle it should be part of the general chart information data. Ironically, all ECS do tell us the tide level of the sounding datum, which in fact we do not need to know.

If the ECS does not report the height datum tide level (MHW on all NOAA charts) then we must refer to the corresponding paper chart or RNC to get it. Generally a hydrographic office uses the same height datum for all of their charts, so reference to any one of them will provide this. With that said, to actually use the height datum for correcting charted heights for tide level, we need to know the actual value of the datum, not just the tide level that defines it.

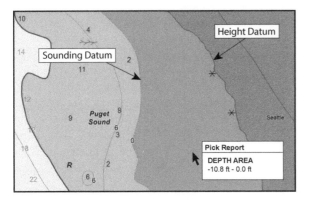

Figure 2.8-2. *How the foreshore on a NOAA ENC defines the two vertical datums. This convenient presentation of the height datum is consistent with* U.S. Chart No. 1, *but this feature may not be available from other ENC sources. (The term "intertidal zone" is sometimes used, but official definitions are not consistent with that term, nor are they with "foreshore." We use the* U.S. Chart No. 1 *definition: the green part of the chart is the foreshore.)*

How we learn this depends on the source of the ENC. The S-57 standard allows for several options. U.S. mariners and others using NOAA charts are again fortunate in that NOAA provides the most convenient solution. According to *U.S. Chart No. 1*, the two contours that define the foreshore (area of the beach that covers and uncovers with the tide) are the sounding datum and the height datum. NOAA includes this height datum contour in the ENCs so we can cursor pick any foreshore to find the local value of the height datum from the depth area report, as illustrated in Figure 2.8-2.

A pick report of the green foreshore (on a NOAA chart) will include a depth area report with two contour values that border the green area. The waterline contour will be 0.0, which is the sounding datum, and the coastline contour value will be a negative number representing the drying height of the coastline when the tide is zero. This is a direct measure of what we want, namely the value of MHW at that location, and thus, the height datum.

On NOAA charts, a value of -10.8 ft, tells us that the value of MHW in this region is 10.8 ft. This is the number we need to compute the height of lights above the water at various tide levels as well as figuring precise bridge clearances. An example with actual data is included in Figure 2.8-1.

With an understanding of the datum based definition of the foreshore borders, we are reminded that what we actually expect to see exposed when underway depends on the tide height. On a negative tide we see more dry land than charted, and in principle we could have less land showing when the tide is higher than MHW. Both effects depend on the steepness of the beach near its limits.

There is one nuance to keep in mind when accessing the MHW data in this manner from a NOAA chart. A small scale chart covers a large area that could include a range in MHW. In South Puget Sound, for example, a 1:80,000 chart covers an area with MHW values ranging from 10.2 ft to 13.8 ft. If you access MHW on this scale you will get the larger value for all locations on the cell, as it is the most conservative when figuring bridge clearances. If you want the more precise value, go to the largest scale chart available for that region, and it will have the local value encoded precisely.

Again, the NOAA solution to the height datum is the most convenient in that we get everything we need from the ENC itself. Other options require tide tables or an RNC to learn the numerical values of the height datum.

The United Kingdom (UK) and New Zealand (NZ), for example, do not encode the actual height datum as the coastline contour. Instead, they mark the coastline boundary of the foreshore with their next highest "standard depth contour" (0, ±2 m, ±5 m, ±10 m...) above the value of the height datum, which is mean high water springs (MHWS) in the UK. In a region where MHWS is 5.7 m, a cursor pick of the foreshore will give a depth area of -10 m to 0 m, because 10 m is the next highest standard contour available. Had the actual MHWS value been 2.5 m, they would encode a -5 m coastline. Using that convention, the results cannot be used for precise tide level adjustments to heights and bridge clearances. It is conservative for all bridge clearances, but not usable for predicting visual range of low lights from low vessels. It has less effect for many lights viewed from the higher decks of ships.

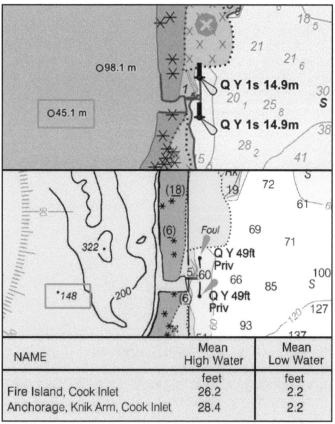

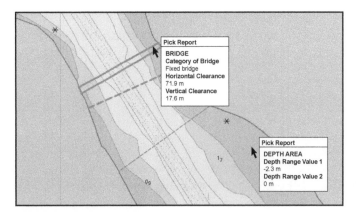

Figure 2.8-3. *Correcting a bridge clearance for MHW found from the foreshore cursor pick. Here MHW = 2.3 m, so if the tide level were 0 m, the clearance would be 17.6 + 2.3 = 19.9 m. That value would be reduced by the actual height of the tide.*

Figure 2.8-4. *Spot elevations near Anchorage, AK (inside the added red boxes) on an ENC (in meters) and RNC (in feet), with charted tide data from the RNC needed to compute MSL.*

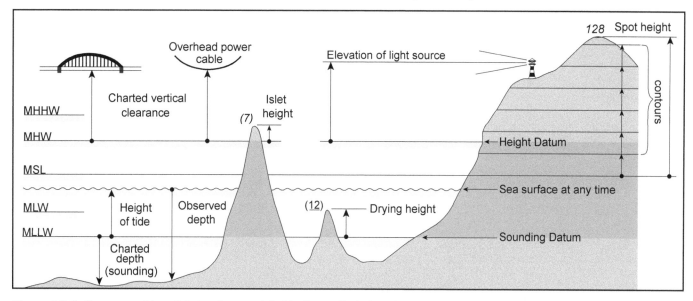

Figure 2.8-5. *Summary of how tide levels are related to the vertical chart datums. Adapted from* U.S. Chart No. 1.

More specifically, the UK uses the above procedure on ENCs with scale bands of 4, 5, or 6. For scale bands of 1, 2, 3 they use a default value of -2 m for the coastline contour on all charts, which is a reasonable estimate for coastal high water levels, and this is rarely crucial when using charts of these small scales.

Canadian ENCs use still another option. They do not encode a numerical value for the coastline contour at all. A cursor pick of any foreshore on a Canadian chart yields one value only, the sounding datum of 0 m. Using Canadian ENCs, it is assumed navigators will refer to the tide tables or paper chart to learn the value of the height datum.

But we are not quite done. Looking at paper charts we would find one more piece of information about vertical datums, namely that contours, summits, and spot elevations on land are relative to *mean sea level* (MSL), which is, for practical purposes, half-way between MHW and MLW. This is indeed another vertical datum! It is the attribute *vertical datum* (VERDAT) choice #3. From a practical point of view, however, this issue is not going to matter much for the use of present generation ENCs. First, ENCs in use now rarely contain elevation contours—their main drawback—and the very few spot elevations presented are generally so high that a small error in datum is a small percentage of the total.

These two vertical datum levels are fairly close. They differ by half the mean range of the tide: MSL = (MHW + MLW)/2, so MHW - MSL = (MHW - MLW)/2. Mean sea level is lower than MHW, so elevations referenced from MSL are slightly higher above the water than the same numerical elevation referenced from MHW. The amount higher is half the mean range of the tide. In Alaska, these differences are up to 15 ft; in Puget Sound near Seattle, the difference is about 7 ft; in much of the world, the dif-

ference is insignificant. A sample of spot elevations near Anchorage is shown in Figure 2.8-4.

A graphic summary of vertical datums on nautical charts is presented in Figure 2.8-5.

2.9 Lights

Lights are the most complex objects in all ENCs. They are the most varied and the most confusing. The complexity stems mainly from the S-52 rules on how lights are to be presented, not the S-57 rules which simply state what information about them must be included in the ENC. And because this is a display issue, we see the most variation between ECS programs on how these are implemented. Depending on the ECS, we see a combination of flares, colored rings, and sector arcs. We must simply learn how our own ECS treats lights, and keep in mind that different ECS programs may have made different choices. Presumably the various type-approved ECDIS have narrower standards on this, but they are inevitably complex.

With that said, we can move on to appreciate that we now have much more information about lights at hand in an ENC than we did on paper charts. This is progress, because lights are crucial to navigation, and also, as noted earlier, an updated ENC is equivalent to an updated *Light List*. In the U.S. these are both updated weekly. Also *light objects* (LIGHTS) in an ENC have essentially all the attributes needed for the light, some of which are not part of the standard paper chart presentation, nor even part of the *Light List* description. Thus, an ongoing virtue of the ENC format is the existence of an attribute placeholder for all the detailed information about a light, even if it may not be filled now. In the future, when the data are known, they will be added. ENCs should just get better with time.

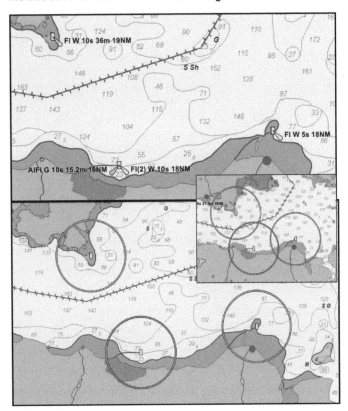

Figure 2.9-1. *Top: One ECS rendition of three major lights in default presentation. **Bottom:** Same lights with "Highlight major lights" turned on. The inset is same as the bottom, but at a display scale zoomed out by a factor of two (then reduced for the inset). This shows that keeping the same symbol size expands the size of the rings relative to the chart. We must be careful in such views not to confuse the extent of the rings with the nominal range of the lights. Note the convention that white lights are shown as yellow flares.*

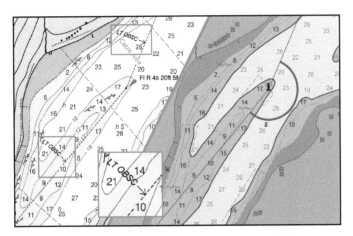

Figure 2.9-2. *Left shows a light on an RNC with notation explaining where the light is obscured. This becomes a sector light on an ENC (right) showing where the light is visible with a prominent arc. The radius of the ring is about 1 inch on the screen, and stays that size regardless of display scale. Click the beacon or light support for a cursor pick, not the ring.*

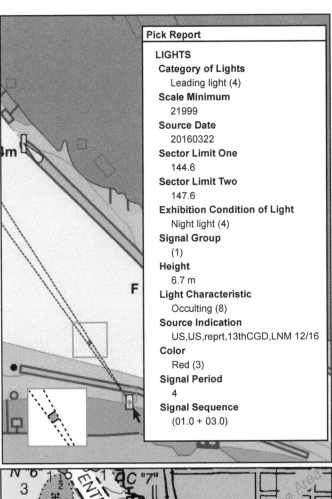

Pick Report

LIGHTS
Category of Lights
Leading light (4)
Scale Minimum
21999
Source Date
20160322
Sector Limit One
144.6
Sector Limit Two
147.6
Exhibition Condition of Light
Night light (4)
Signal Group
(1)
Height
6.7 m
Light Characteristic
Occulting (8)
Source Indication
US,US,reprt,13thCGD,LNM 12/16
Color
Red (3)
Signal Period
4
Signal Sequence
(01.0 + 03.0)

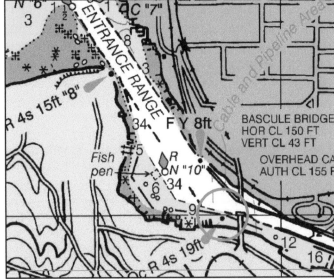

Figure 2.9-3. *A narrow sector light marking an entrance range. This was historically two range lights, but changed to a single narrow one, which can now only be known from the ENC or the Light List; the sector limits are not stated on the RNC! Also the RNC is out of date. According to pick report attribute Source Indication (SORIND) the latest data is USCG Local Notice to Mariners (13th District) week 12 of 2016. That notice reported a slight shift in location and a height change from 19 ft to 22 ft (6.7 m). This change took place during the production of this book. The USCG LNM are all archived online, so these checks are easily made.*

Not counting lighted buoys, discussed earlier, that consistently show a flare (an improvement over the paper chart symbol), we can think of fixed lights in an ENC in three categories: major lights, minor lights, and sector lights. *Major lights* are those with a nominal range of 10 nmi or more (excluding aero-beacon, radio-tower, and Morse-A lights). Less bright lights or lights with unknown range are called *minor lights*. According to *U.S. Chart No. 1*, the default symbol for major and minor lights is a flare. Samples on beacons were shown in Figure 2.7-2.

Some ECS offer the option to highlight major lights, which typically changes the flare to a prominent ring, similar to a sector light with 360° visible range, in the color of the light. Use of this function for a temporary identification of bright lights can be useful, but since the S-52 standard is to maintain symbol size regardless of display scale, these rings can confuse the image on smaller scales. Figure 2.9-1.

A subtlety, helpful to know when correlating *Light List*, *U.S. Coast Pilot*, and chart data, is that the name of a light is usually encoded with the light support object rather than the light object itself. Thus you can get a pick report for a light that gives no name, and a pick report of the beacon with the name "Malina Point Light."

Sector lights have undergone a major change moving onto ENCs. They are now extremely prominent, which is

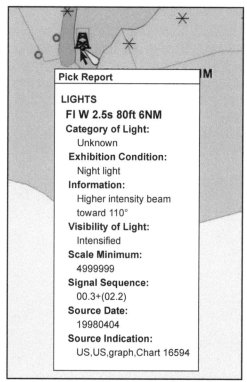

Figure 2.9-4. *Sample of attribute light visibility (LITVIS) and information reports. The pick report shows a common practice of compiling several attributes into a customary light description followed by more specific data. Other ECS reports itemize all attributes as shown in Figure 2.9-3.*

a virtue on larger scale views showing a limited number of them, but this can be a distraction on smaller scales where they can clutter the view. A general guideline for the use of ENCs, is to change display options to best meet your needs at hand. This can call for turning on and off various options on different scales, and the lights display option can be one of those, depending on the ECS.

There is also a minor but valuable philosophy shift in the presentation of ENC sector lights, in that on paper charts, it is often the area where the light is obscured that is emphasized with notes and arcs, whereas ENCs concentrate on the region where the light is visible, as shown in Figure 2.9-2.

Although from paper chart experience, we might have thought of sector lights as having more than one color, on an ENC a sector light can commonly be just one color. Any light that has a known limited range of visibility, large or small, is considered a sector light in the ENC system. Lights on a high coast that are blocked only over the inland side are sector lights, just as are lights with a very narrow visible span used to mark an entrance range. These latter light symbols are difficult to spot, because sector lights do not show a flare at the light location. To get a pick report for the light, we cursor-pick the beacon or related supporting structure. The colored rings of a sector light are not active for pick reports. See Figure 2.9-3.

As noted earlier another change in presentation separates the light itself from the structure that supports it. Thus we can learn more about the structure of the light support from associated parts of the "light symbol," which is often helpful in piloting, using the light structure when the light is not on. Besides beacons, lights can be on an object *landmark* (LNDMRK) or an object *single building* (BUISGL). Both of these have many attributes that describe them for identification from the water. These objects will then include the attribute *function* (FUNCTN) listed as "light support."

One virtue of ENCs is their presentation of multiple identical lights in a column. These are used to mark, among other things, bridge centers, channels through dredge pipelines, and some radio towers. It is difficult to show this graphically on a paper chart, so the presence of such lights is often deferred to chart notes, with no actual light symbol at the location of the light. Such lights are typically not included in the *Light List*. On an ENC, however, a light object can be used with the attribute *multiplicity of lights* (MLTYLT) that specifies the number of identical lights and their vertical or horizontal disposition.

Of frequent interest for navigation in the fog or twilight is the attribute called *exhibition condition of light* (EXCLIT). This can have values (1) on 24h a day, called "light shown without change of character", (2) daytime only, (3) during restricted visibility only, and (4) nighttime only. Most lights are nighttime only, but it can indeed be useful to know if a light is on 24h. This property is listed in the *Light List* for some lights, but not many. Generally we have to assume it is night only, unless this is stated otherwise in the *Light List*. With ENCs, we have a nice place to check this for individual lights. Again, not many are encoded at present, but this is easy information to know, so hopefully it will be filled in for all lights in the future.

Another potentially valuable attribute is *light visibility* (LITVIS). This correlates with the Remarks column in the *Light List*, but it can also be populated on the basis of information in the (weekly) Local Notice to Mariners. It can be applied to any light, but it is not a common attribute. An example is shown in Figure 2.9-4. This attribute can alert mariners if a light is unusually bright or faint, or maybe partially obscured. It is just one more placeholder that, when filled, can add to the description of lights. Similar or supporting data on the light can be included in the attribute *information* (INFORM).

One practice that is new to ENCs is that a light with two colors can be presented as two separate light objects (shown as two flares from the same point). This makes the light descriptions more precise, as it is common for different colors to have different nominal ranges. When using a single flare to represent a light with two colors, NOAA ENCs, like paper charts, display only the shorter nominal range. We have found similar alternating lights encoded both ways.

Although the implementation varies from one ECS to the next, the S-52 standard allows for a cursor rollover display of abbreviated information for lights, buoys, and beacons. This is often the key information needed, without requiring a cursor pick. One very specialized rollover feature seen on just a few ECS programs, is an option to have narrow light sectors extend out from the light, highlighting a range line or a hazard zone the light is marking.

Another ECDIS light feature we have seen in some ECS programs, is a rollover enhancement of the lines marking the boundaries of a sector light. These are generally shown dashed and about one inch long on a typical display, but with this enhanced rollover these lines extend out to the nominal range of the light. This is a subtle change in the display, but a graphic depiction of the nominal range drawn to scale is a useful feature once we understand what we are seeing. Sometimes this feature is a toggle control called something like "enhanced light sectors." We also of course need the height of the light to predict its actual visual range.

White lights have yellow flares

On paper charts all lights are magenta flares, and we learn their colors from the characteristics. On ENCs, red, green, and yellow lights are flares of the appropriate color, but white lights are an exception. They are all depicted as yellow flares or yellow rings in sector lights. It is obviously important that we know this and always check other places

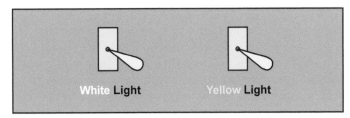

Figure 2.9-5. *White lights show yellow flares. A cursor pick of the left hand one might yield "FL W 6s 21ft 6NM," whereas the right-hand one might read "FL Y 10s." The option to display light labels would clarify this, but that sometimes congests the display. Technically the yellow of the flares should be a slightly lighter shade than that of the beacons, but that is not often detectable on the screen.*

for the color of any yellow light symbol. It could be yellow, or it could be white. (Figure 2.9-5)

Latest *Light List*

As noted, the *USCG Light List* is online for download as a PDF, but there is an almost-hidden nuance to obtaining the latest data. An internet search for "USCG Light List" finds the valuable USCG Nav Center, which has a convenient interactive map of all USCG districts, with the explanation that the *Light List* is updated weekly, and to click any region to download its *Light List*. (In most cases one volume covers several districts.) What you get this way is exactly what is stated at the top of that page: "LIGHT LIST (2017 ANNUAL PUBLICATION)."

This, however, will be an outdated publication whenever you look at it. This is a copy of the edition that was issued in January of that year. The *Light List* is updated every week, but these updates are not in that download. To get the latest data, we must heed the note given that says the updated *Light List* is available on the *Weekly Light List Page*. On that new page, we find two links, one for the new *Light List* body text and one for the front matter and index that does not change. It is difficult to imagine why we might want the outdated version available from the convenient graphic interface. It seems to be there primarily for those third party companies that are downloading this and then selling printed versions.

2.10 Elevation contours and other land features

When we first started to study ENC, we wondered "Where have all the towers gone?" but soon learned that these are now a category of object landmark, and that this was not a big deal. Now, however, we come to what remains a big deal. All navigators are accustomed to using charted terrain for piloting and radar target identification, so the absence of this resource must be considered a drawback to the use of ENCs alone. The conspicuous absence of these contours and other terrain features can be seen in several ENC versus RNC comparisons earlier in the book.

We must, however, keep this in perspective with the tremendous advantages ENCs offer in nearly every other aspect of chart use, and remember we can indeed run both ENCs and RNCs at the same time. In fact, the terrain data we miss from the ENC can even be had from an outdated RNC. The ENCs are quickly and easily updated compared to the RNCs. So we could use ENCs for our up to date charts, and then refer to archived RNCs for the terrain perspective.

Furthermore, the lack of terrain data in present day ENCs (worldwide) is hopefully only temporary. All the objects and attribute structures are in place for showing as much terrain data on an ENC as we are accustomed to on an RNC. Figure 2.10-1 shows how these terrain data could appear within existing ENC.

One reason we do not see contours on U.S. ENCs is that they were first created at a time when the contour data were not available digitally, so adding elevations would call for digitizing the raster chart values. These data are now available digitally, however, so we can hope they will be added in the next generation of charts. Another factor that affects some ENCs is there is an S-57 specified limit of 5 MB per ENC cell and adding the contours could push that limit. Many ENCs, however, are well below the 5 MB limit and they already include extensive depth contours, so it would seem that some or all of the elevation contours

could be added within the existing file-size limits. The fact that elevation contours are all relative to MSL must add some complexity to the issue as well.

Recall from Figure 1.8-3 in Chapter 1 that contours are indeed included on some real ENCs. The example was an ENC from Venezuela. But there is a nuance to that example. Those contours include a scale minimum of 59999. As we zoom out to smaller scales, where they might be better used for piloting, they disappear. Thus there is another complication to adding elevation contours to ENCs, related to displaying them over a broader range of scales, which could call for new guidelines.

We are left with the reality that ENC are the charts of the future and these contours will eventually be sorted out so they are just as useful on ENCs as they are now on RNCs.

Land areas and borders

There is a hierarchy of descriptions for terrestrial parts of any ENC. They are all an object *land area* (LNDARE), and this basic category can have an attribute *object name* (OBJNAM) and/or an attribute *condition* (CONDTN) [options being: 1. under construction, 2. ruined, 3. under reclamation, 4, wingless (wind turbines without blades), or 5. planned construction.] If the attribute *condition* is not provided, then we are to assume it is "normal," which

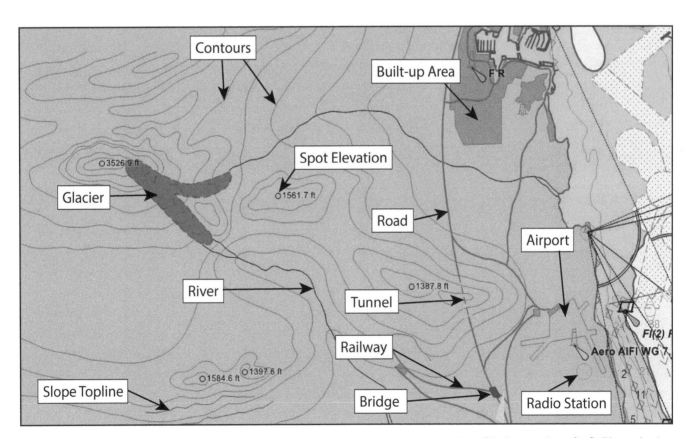

Figure 2.10-1. *Various terrain features that are possible in an ENC, though rarely encoded. This is a section of a fictitious chart GB4X000 from* IHO S-64, Test Data Sets for ECDIS. *Each feature we labeled above can be cursor picked for names and numerical values. See Chapter 4 for other terrestrial feature symbols.*

means: "completed, undamaged and working normally." An isolated island without anything notable about it, would just report as object *land area* with the attribute *object name* = "Jones Island," for example.

The land area, however, could have on it an area of marshland, or something comparable. This is then encoded as an object *land region* (LNDRGN) and this object must have at least one of the attributes *category of land region* (CATLND) or *object name* (OBJNAM). Land region categories are listed in Table 2.10-1. Marshland would be #2.

A land area object could also be overlaid with an object *built up area* (BUAARE), which in turn can have attributes *category of built up area* (CATBUA), *object name* (OBJNAM), and *condition* (CONDTN), among others.

These three objects (land area, land region, and built up area) are singled out here because they are displayed in a very similar manner, as shown in Figure 2.10-2 and 2.10-3. The key is always the cursor pick to learn more of what a bordered area on the land might represent. Notice there are several line styles used for the borders of the land areas in the figures. These each convey information. Solid gray is the normal symbol for a coastline. This is, in principle, where the water would be at MHW.

	Table 2.10-1 Attribute Categories	
	of land region	*of built-up area*
1	fen	urban area
2	marsh	settlement
3	moor/bog	village
4	heathland	town
5	mountain range	city
6	lowlands	holiday village
7	canyon lands	
8	paddy field	
9	agricultural land	
10	savanna/grassland	
11	parkland	
12	swamp	
13	landslide	
14	lava flow	
15	salt pan	
16	moraine	
17	crater	
18	cave	
19	rock column or pinnacle	
20	cay	

2.11 Fairways, traffic lanes, etc

ENC displays of areas with much commercial traffic can become congested quickly as we turn on all the available features, such as cable areas, dredged areas, pipelines, anchorages, various restricted areas, legal boundaries, recommended tracks, traffic lanes, fairways, and more. It is reasonable that mariners choose to hide the features that do not affect their immediate navigation. Of these, however, are three that are crucial to safe navigation at all times, namely traffic lanes, ferry routes, and fairways, when present.

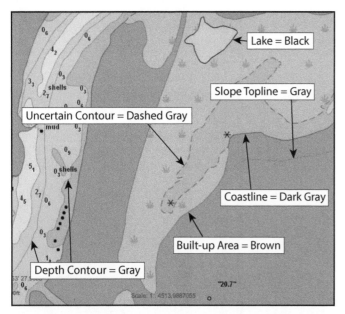

Figure 2.10-2. *Samples of land areas and associated borders. Darker tan areas are object* land area *(no attributes) and object* built up area *with attribute* object name = "Newport Beach." *Lighter tan areas are also objects* land area *(no attributes) plus object* land region *with attribute* category of land region = "marsh." *See Chapter 4, symbols D1 and C23.*

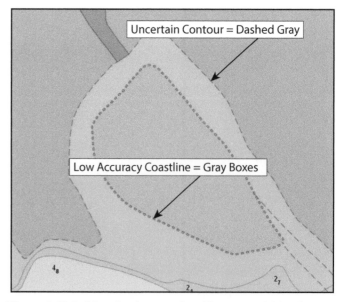

Figure 2.10-3. *More border samples. These special borders only appear when the ENC includes the meta object* quality of data *(M_QUAL). Refer back to Figure 2.4-8. This island is simply identified as a land area, with no attributes or regions.*

In Puget Sound and other busy waterways around the world, knowing where you are relative to the traffic lanes (traffic separation scheme, TSS) is one of the crucial aspects of safe navigation. Rule 10 in the Navigation Rules provides precise instructions on how to interact with traffic following these lanes. Figure 2.12-1 shows a sample of a TSS on an ENC, along with charted ferry routes in the same vicinity. TSS throughout the U.S. are specified in an Annex to the *USCG Navigation Rules Handbook*.

In most ECS programs using RNCs or ENCs, we can manually create a boundary on the chart that provides an alert as we enter a TSS. This practice is discussed in Section 3.13. In some ECS programs, the alerts also apply to ferry routes. The ferries are not following a TSS, but they do follow charted routes, which help navigators plan ahead. The turn that (coincidentally) takes place within the separation zone shown in Figure 2.12-1 is an example.

Fairways are a more subtle feature of the waterway and the *Navigation Rules Handbook*. All narrow channel rules (Rules 9 and 34, and various regulations) apply to fairways as well as narrow channels. Narrow channels are typically obvious from the shape of the waterway relative to vessel maneuverability and they are not identified on charts, but fairways may not be obvious as they could cross open water, and because of this, they are indicated on nautical charts. It is crucial for mariners to understand that the narrow channel rules apply in any charted fairway, even though the water appears to be open. Fairways are typically marked by lateral buoys, but not all buoyed channels are fairways. In some cases, only part of a buoyed channel is a fairway, thus there is a virtue in knowing the chart symbology for them. An example is shown in Figure 2.11-2.

In Figures 2.11-3 and 2.11-4 another fairway is shown as it appears on an RNC compared to an ENC. These important waterways are typically prominent on a paper chart, but sometimes less so on an ENC, depending on the display settings. The extra lines, some bold, some thin,

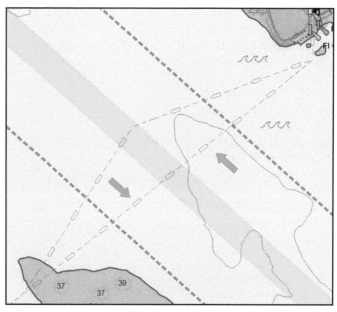

Figure 2.11-1. *Traffic Separation Scheme in Puget Sound. The lanes are 0.5 nmi wide, with a separation zone between them. The arrows mark the inbound and outbound directions. Ship traffic in these lanes can approach 20 kts, with commercial high speed craft traveling at 30 kts. Ferry routes cross the lanes here, but they can also extend into waters well outside of any TSS. Most ECS programs allow alerts to be set to warn of these lanes and routes.*

and the gray color of the lines used on ENCs can obscure the fairway definition, especially when the fairway has been dredged. Furthermore, the apparent line thickness of dashed lines on a computer display can change with the zoom level, which adds to the difficulty in identifying the line symbols when we must distinguish between thick and thin. Symbolized vs. plain boundary styles can highlight the fairways because dredged area boundaries do not change.

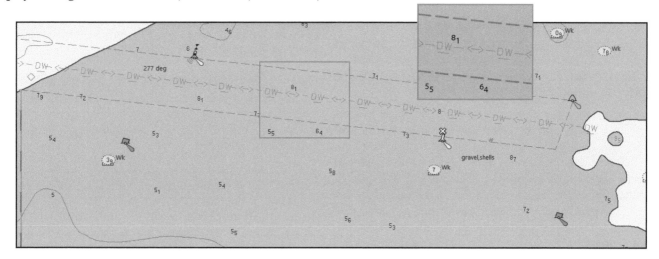

Figure 2.11-2. *A charted fairway, marked by a bold dashed line, that takes up only one half of a buoyed channel. The line labeled "DW" marks the deep water centerline of the fairway. Rule 9 applies within the fairway, but not in adjacent waters of the channel. The insert shows the symbols in closer view.*

Figure 2.11-3. *A charted fairway on an RNC is marked by bold dashed lines. The "tabulation" re-ferred to is a table on the printed chart that specifies the dredged zones of the channel. This fairway appears as open water to boaters in the vicinity without careful chart work, which is all too frequent in these urban inland waters. From chart 18447.*

Figure 2.11-4. *Section of ENC chart covering the same waters as above. Dredged area boundar-ies can confuse fairway symbols. Changing to symbolized boundaries helps, because fairway boundaries change, but dredged area's do not. Dredging is often done in 3 or 4 strips, which add extra lines to the region. U.S. terms for the strips are right outside quarter, right inside quarter, etc.*

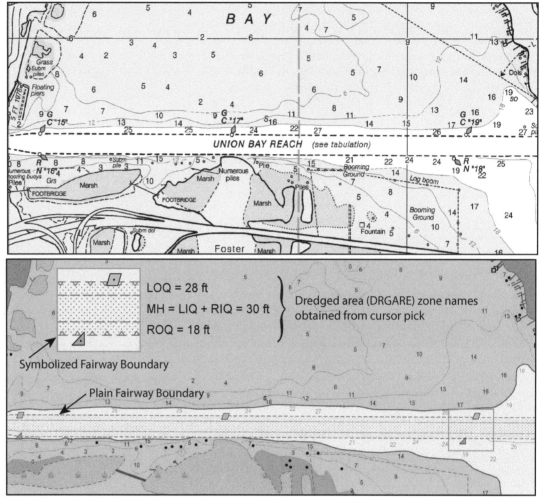

2.12 Chart Text and Meta Objects

When teaching the use of nautical charts, which historical-ly have been paper charts, the first thing we recommend is "reading" the chart. That is meant literally; lay it out flat and read *all* the text on the chart. Much of what is learned will not be used by many mariners, but there will be nug-gets of valuable information and data that we are glad we learned. Doing this for the second, third, and subsequent charts used, gradually takes less time, as we become more familiar the format, but each individual chart has unique information about itself printed directly on it.

This good policy remains valid as we move toward relying on ENCs. The bulk of the chart notes are in text documents included in the exchange set folder, the same place the catalog.031 file and the ENC cell itself, are stored on your computer (discussed in Section 1.6). We can al-ways go directly to that folder to read the text files, but some ECS programs offer "Chart information" links that will display the main text document. Usually, however, the various specialized notes are in separate text documents.

So the recommendation is to scan that main document and then keep in mind that areas with special information are marked with a magenta "i" in a square box. These in-formation symbols, however, also have a *scale minimum* (SCAMIN), so they might not be showing. The surest way to see all notes, is view all text files in the chart folder di-rectly.

Alternatively, another value of having both RNCs and ENCs installed is we can turn off chart quilting, view the RNC, and read the chart notes from the paper chart image itself. This has the additional virtue of showing the tidal data for the chart, which are not all included in the ENC. The main ENC chart information file lists an internet link for tide data (co-ops.nos.noaa.gov), but that website is the figurative equivalent to the Library of Congress of tides—the needed information and much more is there, but it takes a while to find it.

Other general chart information we might care about using ENCs, especially outside of the U.S., is the compila-tion scale of the chart, the equivalent RNC chart number, the date and edition of the chart, and the height datum for the chart. These data are not typically included in the information text files, but are always encoded as *meta ob-jects* within the ENC. These have acronyms that start "M_" such as M_NPUB (nautical publication information) and M_VDAT (vertical datum of data). Some ECS programs extract this data and include it with their own custom "chart information" display. Thus we usually get the compilation scale and the text name of the chart that way. The chart edition and date of issue are usually included with the ECS custom chart information display.

The equivalent RNC number is rarely included, but we can find this several ways. The easy way is to have both installed, then we do not really need it as we can switch back and forth. With only the ENC installed, we can find the equivalent RNC from the descriptive name of the ENC as these are typically the same for RNCs and ENCs— US5WA21M and 18452, for example, are both described as "Sinclair Inlet." Then we can use that name to find the chart in whatever source we are using to obtain the RNC. Another trick would be to cursor pick any light or buoy, and if the ECS displays the attribute *source indication* (SORIND) it will typically include the RNC source, but not many ECS display SORIND.

The tide level of the height datum (discussed in Section 2.8) is not available in many ECS programs, but is readily available in all type approved ECDIS.

2.13 Magnetic variation

We can get spoiled using ECS navigation, because we just push buttons to switch back and forth between magnetic and true directions. In a dark sense, we don't even need to know what the variation is. It is rather like not needing to know how to divide, since we have a calculator in our phone, or how to spell, when there is a spell checker in everything we write with. This is just a small part of the slippery slope of electronic navigation, but still one to be avoided.

Magnetic variation (MAGVAR) is an S-57 object that can be encoded into an ENC as either an area or a point object. Some hydrographic offices include this data, but others (i.e., Canada) do not include it. When present as an area object we can find the value of the variation with a cursor pick at almost any place on the chart. The object has a *scale minimum* attribute (SCAMIN), so it might not be reported on all display scales. On NOAA charts, the SCAMIN value for MAGVAR seems to be the same as used for the soundings, so if you can see soundings you can find the variation.

There is a symbol for magnetic variation seen periodically on the chart, although, as noted, we do not need to click it specifically to get variation. The symbols mark the identifying locations of the various MAGVAR area objects. These are the areas over which the variation is the same within one degree. These symbols are sparse in regions where the variation is not changing by one degree over the geographic span of the ENC cell. At higher latitudes we see more of these, as shown in Figure 2.13-1. There is no correlation between the location of these MAGVAR symbols on an ENC and the placement of compass roses on the corresponding paper charts. On any ENC where we see a lot of

Figure 2.13-1. *Another example of the value of the NOAA Online ENC viewer (Section 1.8), which has the instructive feature of outlining the boundaries of line and area objects when selected. Thus we can see the extent of a MAGVAR area object and the relative location of the symbol. We have made a composite of the reports to illustrate this pattern. In actual use, only one report at a time can be viewed. The MAGVAR areas can have other shapes, and the symbol can be located anywhere within the area, though generally on the meridian central to the area. The inset shows the area object MAGVAR symbol. A hollow version of the symbol marks magnetic anomalies. The acronyms used in the pick report are explained in Figure 2.13-2. The scale minimum attribute of MAGVAR is typically the same as the soundings, so don't expect the MAGVAR object to show up in a report if soundings are not showing.*

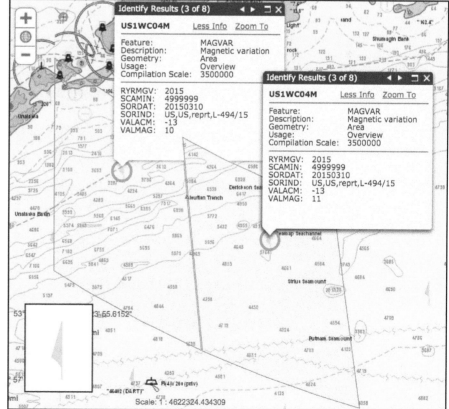

these symbols it means the variation is changing by about 1° between the symbols.

Samples of cursor pick reports for MAGVAR are shown in Figure 2.13-2. This is essentially the same data we get from a compass rose on a paper chart. Often we do not need the value any more precisely, and since we are unlikely to be using old ENCs (as opposed to sometimes using old paper charts) it would be rare we needed to correct for the annual change.

The exception comes when doing a compass calibration, in which case we want this as accurate as possible. The correction is done in the normal manner. Using Sample 1 from Figure 2.13-2, on July 14, 2018, which is 3.33 years after the source date. The correction would be 3.33 x 15' = 50'. The variation is E, correcting to the west, so the corrected value is 19° - 55' = 18° 05', which is essentially 18.0° E.

The main point here is that even though the charts are updated weekly and the computer knows the time and date, we must still treat magnetic variation obtained from an ENC as if we were reading it from a paper chart.

Direct computation of magnetic variation

One reason some hydrographic offices might decide they do not need to encode the magnetic variation is because many ECS programs (and presumably some ECDIS as well) have incorporated special software that can compute the magnetic variation accurately for any location. One example of such a program is *geomag.exe* from the National Centers for Environmental Information (NCEI). This program can be downloaded for personal use, even if not used as part of an ECS. See References.

With this, or a similar program, running in the background, a user can interrogate any location on the chart to obtain the magnetic variation. What information you get from that and how you execute the request depends on the specific ECS that has this feature. It could simply report the variation in plain language or present something similar to an ENC Pick report. When using this supplemental ECS feature for compass corrections, we must double check how it is working. These programs could in principle read the date from the computer and make the rate of change correction.

These details of magnetic variation are important because ship captains are trained to make compass corrections accurate to a few tenths of a degree, which requires correspondingly accurate data.

REPORT 1

Magnetic variation (MAGVAR)

Reference year for magnetic variation (RYRMGV)
   2015

Source date (SORDAT)
   20150310   (= Mar 10, 2015)

Source indication (SORIND)
   US,US,reprt,L-494/15

Value of annual change (VALACM)
   -15   (= 15' W per year)

Value of magnetic variation (VALMAG)
   19   (= 19° E)

REPORT 2

Magnetic variation

RYRMGV	2015	
VALACM	-1	(= 1' W per year)
VALMAG	-11	(= 11° W)

Figure 2.13-2. *Two samples of cursor pick reports for area object* Magnetic variation *MAGVAR from different ECS programs at different locations. The red text was added to clarify the definitions. Attribute* Reference year for magnetic variation *(RYRMGV) is the current year of the World Magnetic Model (WMM2015) that the calculations are based upon. This model is updated every five years. This date will be the same until sometime in 2020. Attribute* Source date *(SORDAT) is the valid time of the variation on this cell. The responsible HO could update the value of the variation and the valid date with a subsequent chart edition. Attribute* Source indication *(SORIND) is a NOAA internal document that references their use of WMM2015. Attribute* Value of annual change in magnetic variation *VALACM is always in arc minutes, with an annual change toward the East being positive, and toward the west negative. The actual value of magnetic variation, attribute (VALMAG) in degrees, is East when positive and West when negative. This value could be specified to the tenth of a degree in some cases. Without the decimal, we have to interpret the value as ± 0.5°. Some ECS programs present all of these conventions in plain language, others are very abbreviated as in Sample 2.*

Chapter 3

Electronic Chart Navigation Underway

3.1 Basic Features and Operations

This chapter discusses some basic procedures that can contribute to safe, efficient navigation using electronic charts. Details and some important background are left to other navigation texts and courses which we have listed in the References. Our focus is on small-craft navigators who are new to electronic charting, but the fundamental procedures are much the same for any vessel. And even though this book is primarily devoted to use of ENCs, for those new to *all* electronic charting it could be best to start with RNCs when first learning to use your chosen ECS. Doing so allows you to concentrate on the tools of the navigation program while using familiar charts. Then later you can take advantage of the benefits ENCs can add to the navigation.

We start with a list of basic features and operations that most ECS programs include, and then discuss how these are used in planning and underway.

• It is crucial to master the loading of new charts into your ECS. Study and practice the process, including auto-update procedures if included, and recall that the auto-update function on some ECS programs only applies to full regions and not individually installed charts. Practice changing between RNCs and ENCs.

• Practice with quilted versus not-quilted chart display. The behavior can differ in RNCs and ENCs. A not-quilted chart shows only one full chart at a time. Some not-quilted displays show paper chart border notes; others show the single chart clipped at the chart area as in Figure 3.1-1. The quilted display shows adjacent charts matched at the boundaries as best can be done. Quilted generally works best, but there are exceptions. Note how displays can change at the border of two quilted charts. Check for options on how adjacent quilted charts with different scales are presented.

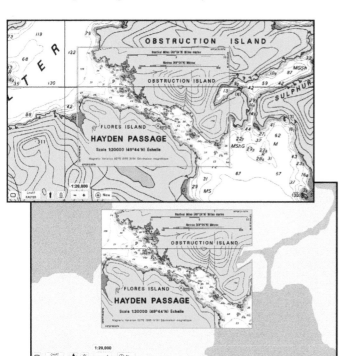

Figure 3.1-1. *Top: Section of Canadian chart 3674 (1:40,000) with a quilted insert of 1:20,000 and chart outlines turned on. Bottom: The not-quilted display of the insert.*

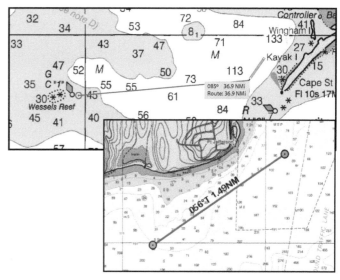

Figure 3.1-2. *Measuring or Range and Bearing tool. Top example is activated by the M key. When an ECS does not offer a specific range and bearing tool, we can always use the new-route tool, which in some cases is preferred as it leaves the data on the screen. Bottom is an example uses the route tool for this type of measurement.*

• Practice measuring range and bearing between two points. Most ECS programs have the option to also measure these from boat to object. We use both tools frequently underway and they are usually two different tools. See Figure 3.1-2.

• Practice setting range rings on marks, waypoints, and the vessel icon itself. There are typically options for the number of rings and the spacing between them. This function has many applications.

• Cursor control in general, and chart zoom and pan control in particular, are fundamental operations. Be sure these are well understood and practiced. In some programs, the mouse works more dependably than a track pad, which means having a place for a mouse on the boat. Also the quality of the mouse itself can affect its operation. Zooming and panning with key strokes might prove to be the safest and most dependable approach underway, so practice with these is valuable, even in light of more convenient mouse control. Learn which, if any, combination of keys can alter the zoom level. A [+] key , for example, could zoom by a factor of 0.2, while [Ctrl] [+] could be a factor of 2 increase. To observe these changes, practice watching the ENC scale bars described in Section 2.7.

• Setting up custom digital data display windows is fundamental to efficient navigation underway. All ECS programs offer options for setting up and saving multiple custom windows for use in different circumstances. The process is more transparent in some systems than others.

• Creating and manipulating user assigned marks and waypoints, and combining these into routes is the backbone of electronic charting. Procedures for setting these up is also one of the things that can differ the most from one ECS to another. Practice is the only solution, including editing by adding or removing points from the middle or ends of the route, reversing the route, hiding or showing marks or routes, and how they are stored or exported, are all key actions that will be done on a daily basis.

• Find the menus that let you do things like change units, and go from Magnetic to True directions. When using Magnetic, it is crucial to check if there is a manual versus automatic setting. The ECS can compute your variation based on the date and your location, but some programs offer the option to enter the variation yourself. When doing that, you have locked in that variation, and if this is done by accident on a long voyage over a notable variation change, you can end up with serious navigation errors. I know of several cases where this threatened the safety of unsuspecting mariners at the end of an ocean passage. It is worth checking once, and setting to automatic.

On ENC cursor pick reports of the variation, the labels E and W are not used. East variation is positive and West variation is negative. (The adage "correcting add east" might serve as a reminder.)

• Remember computer screens can be hard to read in bright sunlight. Practice with a laptop outside in the sunlight to be reminded of this!

3.2 Waypoints and Routes

Using a route made up of a sequence of waypoints is fundamental to navigation. If we are not sailing a route, we are not navigating; we are just out sailing. We may have to deviate from a route without actually changing it, but we must have a route in mind and in the program.

The basic procedure of navigation is to display the course line to the next waypoint, head the boat in that direction, and get underway. Then we monitor the track of the vessel (a bread-crumb trail of past positions) relative to the course line between the last and next waypoint. Our job is to choose the waypoints carefully and then stay on that line, or understand very clearly what we are doing when we leave the line—which we must of course do when tacking under sail. That course line is our guide line to the next waypoint. If the wind or other conditions change, then we can change the waypoints, using as much thought at that stage as when they were first selected.

Sailing in open waters, the route is often just a guide, but we still need it to remain aware of our location relative to the best route we chose earlier. In dangerous waters under power, it can be critical to stay right on the line, zooming in on the screen to detect the first deviation from the course line, and which direction it is in. A visual picture of our actual track deviating from the course line is often a better way to monitor this than just noting differences between COG and the bearing to the next waypoint, or watching a cross track error (XTE) output.

Setting up waypoints is most easily done in stages. First we roughly plot out the general route on a small scale chart showing all or most of the voyage, then we zoom in on a large scale chart to fine-tune the locations. This will entail moving some waypoints and adding others—occasionally using the range and bearing tool to check passing clearances. We obviously want waypoints at each place we change course, but it often helps to add to these with other marks along the route that help monitor progress or to mark specific hazards. Whenever possible, it is best to choose waypoints near some landmark or ATON that is conspicuous, either visually or by radar.

Naming the waypoints is more important than we might guess. Each waypoint name should start with a number, including leading zeros to match the full run in that route. With 15 waypoints, use 01, 02, etc., so that they will sort properly when we transfer them to other devices—or load them into a spreadsheet for archiving or later analysis. Then add a descriptive name to every waypoint. The numbers alone are not enough for safe organization of the route. A sample is shown in Figure 3.2-1.

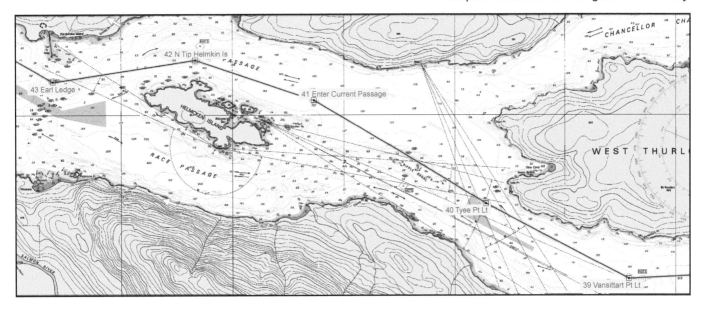

Figure 3.2-1. *Section of a route of waypoints, showing labels with numbers and names.*

Once each waypoint along the route has been named and double-checked as safe and optimum, the waypoint should be locked (an ECS option) so it cannot be moved by mistake.

3.3 Print the Route Plan

Most ECS programs include an option to print out a table of the waypoints that includes not just the name and coordinates of the waypoints, but also the course and distance of each leg of the route. Many include an input for the anticipated speed made good (SMG), and with that, the run time along each leg can be included in the table. With a known departure time, the anticipated clock times at each waypoint can be included. See Figure 3.3-1. Several ECS programs include with this a customized chart image showing the route as well.

These route plans can be printed in the conventional sense (on paper) or they can be printed to a PDF file, which in turn can be transfered to various other computers or mobile devices, including cellphones. The route plan in hand serves as more than a back up; it offers an easy way for multiple users to keep track of the route and look ahead without having to engage the main navigation computer.

3.4 Backup Routes in Mobile Devices

A route plan is a form of backup if the route happens to get corrupted in the main computer, or if the main computer itself has to be replaced. But it would be tedious and slow to enter it all back into the system by hand from a printed list.

A better approach is to export the route in a format that can be directly input to another computer or mobile device. The virtue of having your main navigation route

Victoria to Ketchikan Full
Depart: 2016-06-26 11:00   Total distance: 587.728 nm   Total Time: 4 days 1 hour 58 mins   ETA: Jun 30 12:58

Leg to	Bearing	Distance	Total	Speed	ETA	TTG	Turn	End Position	Notes
▪ 38 Ripple Pt Lt.	303.9° T 286.9° M	2.182 nm	164.895 nm	6.00 kn	Jun 27 14:29	22 mins	36° to port	50°22.485'N 125°34.582'W	
▪ 39 Vansittart Pt Lt	267.3° T 250.2° M	6.560 nm	171.455 nm	6.00 kn	Jun 27 15:34	1 hour 6 mins	29° to starboard	50°22.175'N 125°44.856'W	
▪ 40 Tyee Pt Lt	297.0° T 279.9° M	1.846 nm	173.301 nm	6.00 kn	Jun 27 15:53	18 mins	3° to starboard	50°23.012'N 125°47.435'W	
▪ 41 Enter Current Passage	300.3° T 283.1° M	2.288 nm	175.589 nm	6.00 kn	Jun 27 16:16	23 mins	12° to port	50°24.165'N 125°50.536'W	
▪ 42 N tip Helmkin Is	288.2° T 271.0° M	1.430 nm	177.019 nm	6.00 kn	Jun 27 16:30	14 mins	26° to port	50°24.611'N 125°52.668'W	
▪ 43 Earl Ledge	261.5° T 244.4° M	1.645 nm	178.664 nm	6.00 kn	Jun 27 16:46	16 mins	37° to starboard	50°24.368'N 125°55.221'W	
▪ 44 Hickey Pt Lt	299.1° T 281.9° M	6.835 nm	185.499 nm	6.00 kn	Jun 27 17:55	1 hour 8 mins	17° to port	50°27.689'N 126°04.600'W	
▪ 45 Havannah Channel	282.1° T 264.9° M	10.823 ...	196.322 nm	6.00 kn	Jun 27 19:43	1 hour 48 mins	7° to port	50°29.950'N 126°21.233'W	
▪ 46 Swaine Pt Lt	274.2° T 257.0° M	8.692 nm	205.014 nm	6.00 kn	Jun 27 21:10	1 hour 27 mins	13° to starboard	50°30.593'N 126°34.862'W	
▪ 47 Blinkhorn Lt	288.2° T 271.0° M	7.895 nm	212.909 nm	6.00 kn	Jun 27 22:29	1 hour 19 mins	5° to port	50°33.058'N 126°46.661'W	
▪ 48 S Tip Cormorant Is	282.9° T 265.6° M	5.265 nm	218.174 nm	6.00 kn	Jun 27 23:22	53 mins	14° to starboard	50°34.230'N 126°54.740'W	
▪ 49 Alert Rk Lt	297.4° T 280.2° M	1.769 nm	219.943 nm	6.00 kn	Jun 27 23:39	18 mins	14° to port	50°35.045'N 126°57.212'W	

Figure 3.3-1. *Section of a route plan. There are many variations of these among ECS programs. They can be printed or exported to a spreadsheet for customizing the display. An average SMG can be used for time estimates, or make several route plans with different SMGs. These can also be updated along the voyage.*

in a working handheld GPS is obvious. If something goes wrong at a crucial time, you can switch to it and carry on. Furthermore, having the active route in a handheld allows the navigator and other crew to keep track of position along the route, even when the main navigation computer at the nav station is functioning properly.

There are several proprietary file formats for route transfer that work with specific mobile devices, but the generic format that works with essentially all of them is called GPS exchange format (GPX), so we would export the route to a file called, for example, Victoria-Ketchikan. gpx.

This file then serves as both a backup to the route in use, as well as a way to move the route to handheld GPS units. A key part of learning practical, safe electronic navigation is to practice exporting a route and then loading it into your portable device of choice. The latter step often calls for a special computer app made by the portable device company that facilitates the transition. In some cases, you can just copy the file to an SD card that the device can read.

This exercise of moving a route from computer to portable device is more than just a backup step in some applications. For those who do their primary electronic navigation by tablet device, this can be a key step to routine preparation, because it is usually much easier to shape a route in a computer than it is on a small handheld device. It does not matter that the device may be using a different set of echarts, we are working here only with the routes. It is easier to zoom and pan the charts in a computer, as well as view tidal current flow patterns which are often part of

a computer based ECS. Then with the comfort and better viewing of the computer, we can set up all of our routes, export them, and load them into the portable device for navigation underway. For this application, you can often email the GPX file to yourself as an attachment, and then open the attached GPX file to the nav app.

If you happen to be working with an ECS that does not offer a thorough route plan option, the GPX file can be converted to a CSV file (comma separated values) with third party apps so it can be viewed in a spreadsheet program.

3.5 Practice with Dual Screen Display

There is much to be gained from a dual display of two charts, viewed side by side. A common setup underway would be to have one display of a smaller scale chart showing your general location in a broader view of the waterway, and then a larger scale, or zoomed-in view, of your vessel for monitoring close traffic or to watch your track more carefully in changing current or wind. The broad view helps you identify landmarks on the horizon that may not be on the close-up view in use.

Your vessel icon will show up on both sides, so range and bearings to a wider array of targets is possible without changing the screens. Some ECS programs have single button control of the screen layout, others put this in a menu; some ECS programs do not offer the dual screen option at all.

With both ENCs and RNCs installed, you can load an ENC on one side, and the RNC of the same region and magnification on the other, for what is effectively an on-

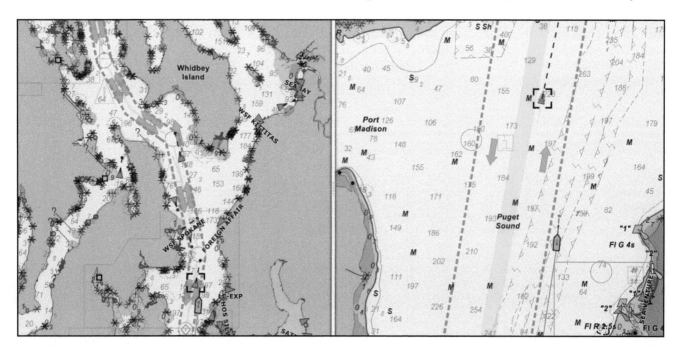

Figure 3.5-1. *Dual displays of vessel position showing larger scale on the right to monitor traffic and progress and smaller scale view on the left for location awareness. When an RNC is also available, it could be used on the left for better terrain perspective, while using the enhanced information available on the ENC for more immediate navigation.*

going lesson on charting. This dual view will invariably reveal valuable insights into both the ENC and the RNC. Even without dual screen, you can make this important comparison by switching chart types, which is typically a quick process in most ECS programs, but the dual screen makes it easier.

With both ENCs and RNCs installed you can take advantage of the best aspects that each has to offer (from your perspective). An example is shown in Figure 3.5-1. You may find certain details of a light from a cursor pick of the ENC that are not apparent from the RNC, and in many cases, the cleaner display of the ENC is better suited than that of the RNC. When elevations of the nearby terrain are crucial for piloting, use the RNC, as this information is mostly missing from the ENC. Other advantages of loading both formats are discussed in Section 3.13.

3.6 Instrument and Navigation Data Displays

All ECS programs offer ways to display digital data of your choice in a separate window or fixed panel at the side of the screen. In modern ECS programs we can display just about any data we choose, because most sensors on the boat are tied into the National Marine Electronics Association (NMEA) data string that feeds the program. Often, the shape, size, and location of the displays can be adjusted.

Underway, on a selected route, we typically want the minimum needed in prominent view, meaning visible some distance away from the computer screen. The present GPS position is one thing we want ready access to, but we must be careful setting this up. We typically have two positions we can display, the present GPS position of the vessel or the present position of the cursor on the screen. These position displays might even look identical in the

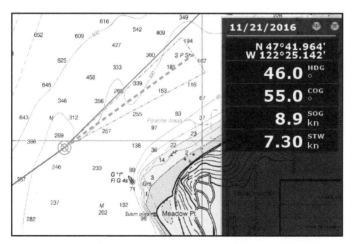

Figure 3.6-1. *Sample data display, showing the effect of current on vessel motion. The vessel icon is an ECDIS style; blue line is vessel track; green line marks vessel heading; thick red dash is a 6-minute COG predictor, and the thin red dashes mark an anti-grounding cone. Each of these ECS features is discussed in following sections.*

display panel, depending on the ECS. Any risk of confusion at all should be rigorously avoided. Potential errors are obvious.

Even systems that prevent this in the instrument data panel still offer a digital display of the cursor position elsewhere on the screen, and for good reason; we very often want to use the cursor to identify an object or vessel on the chart. Such a simple potential confusion illustrates the importance of good communications amongst those using the ECS.

Beside our present GPS position, we also want to be aware at all times of the vessel heading (HDG) and the course over ground (COG). The vessel heading display requires a separate heading sensor, which is common on modern vessels, and is also used for the radar display and autopilot controls.

The COG is the most important number in our active navigation, as it tells which way we are actually moving—the HDG just tells us which way we are pointed. When HDG and COG do not agree, we are being set off course by wind or current, assuming the heading sensor is properly calibrated.

A proper comparison of HDG and COG, or any other sensor reading for that matter, such as SOG (speed over ground), STW (speed through the water or knotmeter speed) or wind speed and direction, brings up a crucial point in the ECS setup. Many ECS programs include the option to average any sensor input over some time period. Thus instead of reading a changing COG every second or so as we swing about in a seaway, the ECS can average this over a period of a few seconds or longer. In many applications a smoothed out reading is more useful, in other applications an averaging we do not know about could be very misleading. So it is important to learn how this is done and set in your program.

The SOG is another parameter that is useful to watch, but the COG is the most crucial as it tells us if we are getting into trouble. The SOG just tells us how fast we might be getting into trouble.

Other common data to display might be the bearing to the next waypoint (BWP, our desired course) and maybe time to next waypoint (TTG). The accuracy of the computed TTG to the next waypoint, or indeed an overall ETA for the route of several waypoints, naturally enough depends on how well we can maintain our course. If we are holding course, these displayed arrival times are useful data, but if we cannot hold the course, these precisely stated time estimates can be misleading. How much the ETAs are wrong depends on how far off course we are and on our ability to get back on course. For an accurate ETA, we must reset our course to one we can follow.

The TTGs and ETAs computed in an ECS are based on a derived parameter, the velocity made good (VMG). It is the speed made good in a particular direction, usually the direction to the next waypoint, in which case it is sometimes called VMC, for velocity made course. This distinguishes it from the common use by sailors, who use "VMG" to mean speed made good in the direction of the true wind. Figure 3.6-2 illustrates the effect of VMC on the TTG to the next waypoint.

When under sail, VMC and VMG are important parameters to monitor to detect changes in the wind and current, which affect routing choices such as when to tack or jibe, or deciding which is the favored side of the wind. Even though the ETA or TTG will be off when based on VMC, a sudden change in the environment will cause a sudden change in one or both of these parameters. Likewise comparing them on each side of the wind helps determine favored tack or jibe.

ECS programs are not consistent on the terminology for VMG, so it is important to learn how your own program handles this, and to be aware that the next program you use could be different. Programs that do not offer *both* VMG-wind and VMG-course, will generally use "VMG" to mean VMG-course, which others call VMC.

Remember that accurate VMG-wind requires accurate true wind data. Some ECS programs that compute true wind based upon apparent wind measurements offer the

option of using COG and SOG or HDG and STW for the vector solution. When using the former, we get true wind in the normal sense, relative to the ground; when using the latter we get wind relative to the moving water, which is sometimes called "water wind," implying the name "ground wind" be used for true wind. When the water is not moving, these two winds are the same.

Sailors can also choose to display various wind parameters within the ECS they are using. In some tactical and performance ECS programs, display of wind data is crucial, because it is also used for dynamic weather routing. In other cases under sail, there is enough wind data display in other instruments to remove the need for a duplicate display within the navigation program.

Some navigators are accustomed to navigating by the cross track error (XTE). This is a digital or graphic display telling you how far you are off of the course line, and in which direction. Displays of XTE can be purely digital, or in various graphic formats.

The best choice of what to display and how to display it depends on the circumstances. Generally you will want to predefine and save several display windows, and then show them as needed. This choice also depends on how far you must be from the actual screen when navigating or

Figure 3.6-2. *Various derived parameters that can be displayed in a navigation information panel. Here we have a sailing vessel tacking to a mark (green flag) 2 miles into the wind (blue arrows). VMG is the SOG projected onto the direction of the wind. This remains constant so long as the wind remains constant. The VMC (red) is the SOG projected onto the direction to the mark, which changes as the vessel proceeds. The displayed ETA is based on VMC, which becomes less accurate with time, because under sail this boat cannot proceed in that direction. When it tacks its SOG will remain about the same, and the COG will change (in this example) roughly 100°. Assuming wind and current remain constant, the VMG would be a better guide to the ETA. ECS programs designed for sailing performance can solve the ETA issues fairly precisely. Under power, an ETA based on VMC is more often usable, but we must remain aware of how it is computed.*

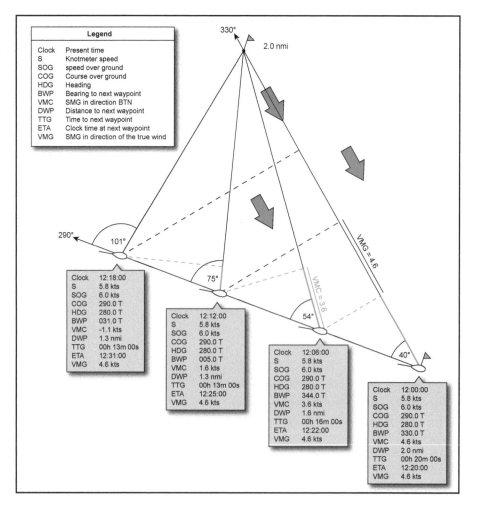

driving the boat. In some cases you do not actually have to see details on the chart, so long as you have large, clearly visible values of COG, SOG with bearing and distance to the next waypoint in view. Other times, you will want to be up at the chart, fine tuning the course, checking for current set, and so on, in which case you may choose to display more parameters in smaller fonts.

Given sufficient sensors on the vessel, you can also display such things as ship's battery power, fuel consumption, even fridge temperature. On some ECS programs, there is an option to display a live camera view looking aft, or elsewhere. Sailing in places like the Gulf Stream, a prominent display of the sea water temperature can be a crucial aid to your navigation.

As noted in Section 2.2, the ECS you choose could have generic user interface modes called "navigation" versus "planning," or two alternative names for these. The so called navigation mode could limit what you wish to display, or how you wish to display it, when actually navigating, but most ECS programs allow you to navigate in either mode, even if they at first automatically switch to navigation mode when a live GPS signal is detected.

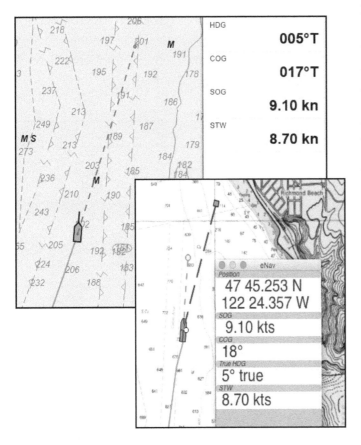

Figure 3.7-1. *Vessel icons with heading and COG-prediction lines from two different ECS programs for a vessel in current, causing the COG to be different from the heading. The marker at the end of the longer dashed lines shows where the vessel will be in 6 minutes if both SOG and COG remain constant.*

3.7 Configuring Your Vessel Icon

Beside displaying a track of past positions, an ECS offers two graphic ways to monitor motion at any moment from your own vessel icon itself. Two important graphic embellishments we can add to the vessel icon are a heading indicator and COG predictor (Figure 3.7-1). These options are always present, but their implementation and appearance varies amongst ECS programs.

The heading indicator is a short line extending from the head of the vessel icon that is parallel to the center line. This line enhances our awareness of the direction the boat is pointed, which may not be obvious from a small icon, or especially one that is not shaped like a vessel. In some programs the heading indicator is a fixed length, in others you can set its length in nautical miles. This indicator will point in the direction of the heading sensor input. In certain ECS programs, the heading line extends clear across the chart.

In the presence of wind or current, however, the vessel may not move in the direction it is headed. It will be crossing the chart in the direction of the COG. All ECS programs include the important option to display a COG prediction line on the vessel icon that marks where the vessel is predicted to be at some user-selected time in the future.

In contrast to the heading indicator, the COG predictor is a dynamic variable, because we can set it to show the predicted location at any projected time period. In close quarters moving slowly this might be down to a 1-minute look ahead, or even less, but in open waters or on smaller-scale charts we might choose a 1-hour interval, or longer. Oftentimes, a look ahead of 6 minutes is useful, because then the predictor line extends forward for a distance equal to one tenth of the vessel speed. When using a long look-ahead in open waters, we would want to switch to a shorter predictor if traffic appears.

Figure 3.7-2 shows the official ECDIS vessel icons along with these two predictors. The heading line is a plain short segment (with option for a cross-chart projection); the COG predictor is marked by a double arrowhead with an option of six tick marks at user-selected time intervals.

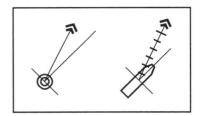

Figure 3.7-2. *Official ECDIS own-ship icons, with COG and heading predictor lines. Most ECS programs use a vessel shaped icon of fixed size. The scaled vector icon matches the dimensions of the vessel, visible on large scale displays. There are also ECDIS options to these displays, some using a heading line that extends across the chart.*

Another embellishment of the vessel icon is the addition of range rings, centered on and attached to the moving vessel. Use of these is discussed in Section 3.9. Most ECS programs also offer the option to input own-ship dimensions, and then display a scaled representation of the vessel on large-scale or zoomed displays. This option is discussed in Section 3.12 on AIS targets, which have a similar scaled-vessel icon display.

3.8 Tracking Options

The displayed tracks of past positions is a crucial component of electronic navigation. Without tracks, we know where we are on the chart from location of the vessel icon, but just knowing where we are is not nearly as valuable as knowing how we got there. Even with a COG predictor showing where we are going at the moment, we still need the track to show how we got there.

The COG predictor is an *instantaneous* prediction of our motion, but it does not tell us our past course made good (CMG). We could be, for example, in a localized current eddy that shifts the COG predictor well off of our recent track line, and without that track we would not know that. The observation that the COG predictor is no longer in line with the track tells us something has changed, and we learn this at a glance—provided we have the track displayed.

Furthermore, the plotted track is the most sensitive way for early detection that we are not making good what we are steering. In principle, we see this from the digital displays of HDG and COG, but in any seaway or windy conditions we may not be steering a steady course, so the HDG and subsequent COG bounce around digitally. It takes some time to do a mental average of these to detect they are diverging. But the plotted track averages out these variations, so we can see the track line pull off of the course line (when zoomed in on the vessel) faster than we get digital warning from the displayed values.

A first step in setting a new course is to zoom in on the vessel icon and watch the track to see if it is on course or not. Then, if necessary, make minor adjustments in heading, to find the right one to steer to stay on course. Then we can zoom back out for a more normal display.

Thus we see how important it is to understand how the ECS has been configured with regard to the track display. This display can usually be set to plot a mark at some selected time interval or after some distance run. That is, plot a point every 5 seconds, or every 5 minutes; every 100 yards, or every mile, etc. How we set this best depends on what we are doing at the time. If we set these track points more frequently than needed, we can end up with very large files of stored tracks. On the other hand, if the steps are too far apart, we miss details that could be crucial to safe navigation. Transiting a narrows of strong, swirling currents, we want as detailed a track as possible. Crossing the ocean we do not need such small increments.

One of the steps in learning a specific ECS is learning how the tracks are configured and how to change this. If you choose to save a track, you may have the option, once again, to select how it should be configured. Tracks can

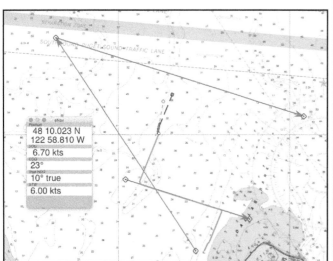
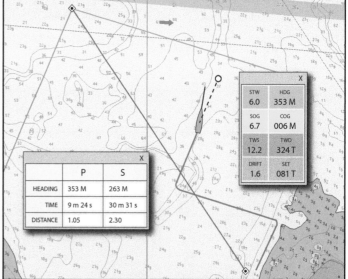

Figure 3.8-1. *Using an ECS to plan a sailing layline to the next mark. Left is a basic solution without any special computations—i.e., once the windward tracks are established, we can find the reverse heading along each tack with a route tool, and then manually draw in the final leg (layline) to the mark with another route line. Then use the measuring tool or the COG predictor to find time to the layline. The blue lines are manually drawn one-leg routes. This is quick and easy with any ECS. For comparison, on the right is a schematic showing only a fraction of what can be computed and incorporated into the routing display using a sophisticated sailboat routing ECS. This one computes and displays the laylines automatically, and then rotates them as the wind shifts.*

then be converted to routes for use in the future, or you can just load and display the saved track, and set a new route with the past track in view. When under sail, you will thus recall what tacking or jibing angles you had when you were there before. For racing sailors, a history of past tracks will remind you of persistent lifts or headers in specific regions, and thus accelerate your accumulation of local knowledge.

Sailors can also use the lay of the track lines on opposite tacks to predict the layline to the next waypoint, taking into account current and leeway, as shown in Figure 3.8-1. How you actually make the parallel-rulers-style move of the line depends on the ECS. In some systems you can draw a range and bearing line, then just grab it and move it; without that option, you would read the bearing along the line, then draw another one emanating from the target waypoint.

3.9 Vessel Icon Range Rings to Aid Radar Watch

Beside putting range rings on charted marks as piloting aids, or on waypoints as arrival markers, or on our anchor location to warn of dragging, we can also add range rings to the vessel icon itself. The vessel icon rings can be used for monitoring minimum distance off in piloting, or you can match the rings on the vessel icon with those on the present radar display for an effective way to interpret the radar screen. This is most useful for vessels that have a radar but not a radar interface to the ECS. Many ECS systems offer a full radar overlay option that plots the actual radar image right on the chart in use, but this in turn calls for a compatible radar and associated connections or ECS enhancements.

A display of the vessel rings alone might even be preferred in cases when the overlay of actual signals might clutter the image. Figure 3.9-1 shows an example of using these rings on an ECS that does not have a radar overlay option installed, compared to what the actual radar image looks like from that location.

3.10 Check the Charted Position

The two hallmarks of good navigation are looking ahead and not relying on any single source for crucial decisions. The COG predictor and anti-grounding cone contribute to the former, but to meet the latter we must periodically check the GPS position. GPS is remarkably dependable,

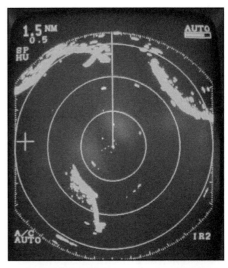

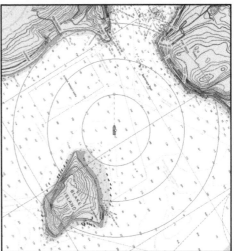

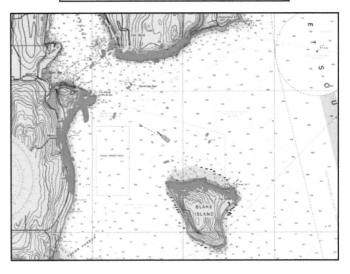

Figure 3.9-1. *Top is a radar image in head-up mode with range rings at 0.5 nmi. To help interpret the radar image, we can set matching range rings on the vessel icon in the ECS (set to course-up display) as shown in the middle view. This display is possible in the most basic ECS, and from the overlap of the rings we learn what we are seeing on the radar, independent of visual identification. The steep terrain of the targets limits the radar images to the front face of the targets. This is effectively a low-budget alternative to a more sophisticated system that overlays the radar image on the chart within the ECS, as shown in the bottom panel. In a busy radar image, the middle option can sometimes be preferable to the full overlay, which can obscure the chart.*

and as such is often taken for granted, but there are several processing steps between a GPS antenna and a displayed vessel position on the electronic chart—not to mention that a GPS fix is indeed not infallible.

Certified ECDIS has built in several checks on this, but a common ECS we might be using will not likely have these safeguards. The input could be perfectly valid, but your vessel icon is no longer moving, or the GPS signal was lost and the ECS switched to a DR mode that is advancing the position based on some other inputs.

In short, a responsible navigator should periodically use traditional piloting or other confirmations of the vessel position shown on the chart. There are numerous ways to do this, ranging from very fast to very accurate.

Position checks underway

(1) Look around for quick visual confirmation. Passing a headland or light beacon at an estimated distance off is an easy check. Passing a buoy is also fast, but less dependable as the buoy may be off station.

(2) Check if the measured sounding is consistent with your charted location. In areas of large tides, this reminds us to have tidal data handy, or how to access it from within the ECS.

(3) Check radar for a prominent range and bearing target and compare radar values with the quick values we can read from the ECS using its range and bearing from vessel tool. See Figure 3.10-1.

(4) Smaller vessels without radar can take compass bearings to several points and plot them electronically in the ECS using the route tool. Or just do a quick check of two landmarks with the bearing tool, and mark the position as confirmed.

(5) Sailing on a natural range, or with the heading line on a prominent target that makes the course line an LOP, we can check off our progress with single bearing LOPs near the beam as we pass them.

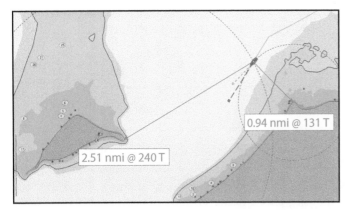

Figure 3.10-1. *Using ECS range and bearing tool (red arrows) to check GPS position. Also shown is the option for quick easy plotting of radar range measurements using the ECS range ring tool (green circles), centered on the radar target.*

0.94 nmi @ 131 T

2.51 nmi @ 240 T

(6) For more precise checks with radar we can measure several ranges and plot them in the ECS with range rings on marks placed at the radar targets. We will be moving when we do this, so as with any running fix, we want to measure first the LOP (or COP) that is changing more slowly. Thus with two bearings, we take the one ahead or astern before taking the one near the beam. With COPs, this sequence is reversed.

After making such a position check, it is good practice to document when it was done. When navigating by paper charts, we always teach what we call "Rule No. 1," namely plot your position on the chart frequently, and label it with the time. "Frequently" depends on the circumstances. In quickly changing, hazardous waters, this could mean as fast and often as you can; in the open ocean this could be every few hours. It does not matter how you got the fix, but it should be a fix, not just a DR position. With a plot of these positions on the paper chart, we see at a glance what we need to know, our actual CMG. And since we have times recorded, we can compute our SMG, or just use the time interval plotted to move our position forward with dividers.

When using an ECS, much of this is done for us automatically, in that we see our COG and SOG and have the track of positions. Usually there is an option to save the track, in which case it is converted to waypoints, and in that table you have times on the track positions. But these data are not confirmed positions; they are the GPS positions. And recall that the displayed COG and SOG are instantaneous values, not values made good over some time or distance.

Thus it is good practice when transitioning into electronic chart navigation, that we keep a record of the positions we actually confirmed. There are several ways to do this. As noted above, if you do the plotting for the visual or radar piloting fixes, you can leave the LOPs and COPs in place on the display, or select a specific mark icon that you will use to indicate a confirmed position fix. All ECS programs allow for the placing of a custom mark (as opposed to a waypoint), and the icon for that mark can be selected from a large set of icon designs. Thus, we might choose one of those designs to represent a confirmed position fix and place one at each confirmed position along the track. Then be sure to label it with the time, and we are back to meeting Rule No. 1 with the electronic charts.

This procedure provides a more rigorous confirmation of your navigation if that should ever be needed, and it provides a confirmed location to initialize the DR mode of your ECS if the GPS signal is lost for any reason. Most ECS programs have the option to plot your DR track on the screen based on either manually input speed and heading, or sensor based data, without GPS data. It is obviously crucial to know if you are in DR or GPS mode at all times, and to note the behavior of your ECS in this regard. Some systems offer a DR mode whenever the GPS signal is lost.

And of course we should not forget the traditional solution of making a (paper) logbook entry each time a position is confirmed, which remains sound practice. We sadly, however, hear of diminishing paper logbook use as mariners rely more on electronic solutions.

3.11 Confirm Current Predictions

Another tenet of good navigational philosophy is staying in charge. One element of that in areas of notable current flow is to do your best to predict the currents that lie ahead and then check to see how good these predictions were as you proceed. If they pan out, we are more or less in charge; to the extent they are wrong, we need to figure out why. The same can be said of the wind and sea state, discussed briefly in Section 3.15.

Current Measurement

Some ECS programs will do the current measurement computations for us providing we have inputs to the ECS from a knotmeter (for speed through the water, STW) and a heading sensor (for heading, HDG). Then the ECS solves

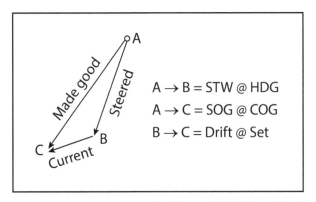

Figure 3.11-1. *Vector solution for Set and Drift. When the boat moves from A to B, the water moves from B to C, which yields the motion over the ground A to C.*

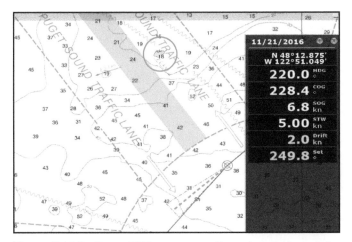

Figure 3.11-2. *Some ECS programs offer automated current computations, as shown here. The nearest current prediction station for comparison underway is circled in red.*

for the vector difference between course steered and course made good to determine the current that caused the difference between them, as shown in Figure 3.11-1.

With the required inputs and automatic computations, we can display the dynamic values of set and drift in an instrument panel, as shown in Figure 3.11-2. Knotmeter and heading sensor, however, must be carefully calibrated to obtain useful results, otherwise we can be lead astray by this convenient output.

Without heading and speed input to the ECS, we can still read HDG and STW from the instrument's own displays, and solve the vector triangle manually on a maneuvering board. Or better still, solve the vector triangle with the plotting tools available on the ECS screen. An example is shown in Figure 3.11-3. The steps are:

(1) Create a one-leg route from any point on the screen that is in the direction of your HDG, with a length equal to your STW—or some easy fraction of it, depending on chart scale, such as STW/2 or STW/10. We are drawing a line length equal to how far we would move in 1 hr, 30 min, or 6 min. Moving very slowly, it could be convenient to make it 2 x STW.

(2) Then from the same starting point, create another one-leg route in the direction of recent average COG, with a length equal to the recent average SOG, using the same scale you chose for the STW line.

(3) Then use the measurement tool to find the range and bearing from the end of the HDG line to the end of the COG line. The direction of that line is the set of the current and length is the drift in the scale used.

For programs that let you draw and move a range and bearing line, you might be able to use the COG and heading

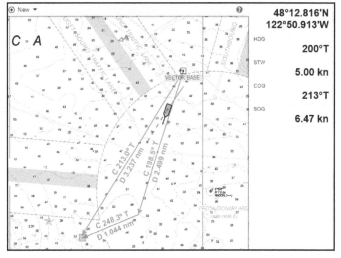

Figure 3.11-3. *An ECS that offers movable range and bearing lines. Using a 30-min run scale for the vector lengths, the current is found to be 2.1 kts toward 248° T. Here we used approximate values by just drawing the vector lines parallel to the vessel icon's heading and COG predictor.*

predictor lines to orient the vectors, which could save time in setting them numerically—this solution does not need to be super precise because the predictions themselves are only some ± 15% accurate on average, not to mention that the predictions apply to the specific location of the reference station, not to a point that is, say, 200 yards away from it.

Note that the "current" found this way is not necessarily all do to true motion of the water. Leeway, helm bias in a seaway, and sensor errors can each contribute to this in varying degrees. What we are measuring is the effective "error current" we need to know to understand and project our navigation. (Indeed, if we see a significant error current when we know for certain there is no water current, we can use the results on different headings and speeds to study the source of the errors.)

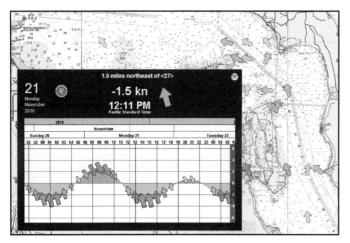

Figure 3.11-4. *Sample of live and forecasted current predictions at official stations from within the ECS. Most ECS programs have such a presentation.*

Figure 3.11-5. *Sample of high resolution current forecasts presented in an ECS that is popular for its sailing performance and routing prowess.*

In areas with significant (real) current flow, however, this is the best we can do to check that the current predictions are about right, and with the powerful tools of ECS we have easy and continual access to the official predictions.

Current Predictions in ECS programs

ECS have revolutionized our access to official tide and current predictions. Both can be fairly accurately predicted on the basis of constant numeric parameters for many parts of the world. Most ECS programs use these parameters to compute and display tide and current predictions at each of the reference stations and subordinate stations along a waterway. The results are displayed with scaled current arrows and tide gauges located at their proper places on the chart. Click one for a time plot of their behavior. Stepping forward in time, you can watch tides and currents change to help plan routes sensitive to either. The tide and current display has nothing to do with the charts, ENC or RNC, and can be overlaid on either format. A sample is shown in Figure 3.11-4.

For any location along a planned route, we can check the predicted current speed and direction with a button click, and shape our route accordingly. This ECS functionality is indeed one of the attractive features of electronic navigation in areas of notable current flow. In fact, this feature is so valuable for small craft mariners it justifies using a computer for the route setup, even if the final goal is to transfer the route to a handheld GPS or tablet for actual navigation underway.

For the safest current predictions in areas where they matter, we should spot check the ECS predictions (which are based on data stored in the individual ECS) with the most recent official predictions from NOAA, or the equivalent HO in other parts of the world. Needless to say, no ECS manufacturer guarantees that their current predictions are right. A spot check or two also confirms that you understand the timekeeping system the ECS is using for this. This could be local to your vessel icon location, or local to where you are planning the route, corrected for daylight savings time or not, and so forth. It has to be checked at least once.

Some ECS programs can incorporate the current predictions into route planning automatically on some level. In selected inland areas there are high resolution current predictions available as shown in Figure 3.11-5. These can be further interpolated for automatic route optimization in some programs. GRIB (gridded binary) formatted ocean model current predictions are available online from several sources, discussed further in Section 3.15. There are also isolated buoys that report live current predictions that are ideal checks of any forecast. Several sources are listed in the References.

When sailing in coastal waters with an internet connection, mariners can access live current measurements from HF-radar in most U.S. coastal waters and selected areas around the world. The data are for visual planning and checking. These data cannot yet be fed into an ECS. Measurements extend up to 90 nmi offshore, and where available are potentially the best current resource. Easily accessed recent data from these sites help us make our own forecasts. Needless to say, we are never guaranteed adequate connections, nor do the stations guarantee to be online, so we must keep our traditional sources at hand.

3.12 AIS Target Display

Even the most basic ECS programs now includes the display of AIS targets detected by an onboard AIS receiver. There are thousands of vessels with an AIS receiver that are not required to have the more expensive AIS transceiver to broadcast their own positions and data—although the latter enhances safe navigation for any vessel. The ability to display and monitor AIS traffic and AIS marked aids to navigation (ATON) in an ECS is a primary contribution to safe small-craft navigation. Most ECS programs display AIS targets on the screen much like they are shown on type-approved ECDIS, with only slight variations in style. Differences that do arise are rarely distracting, and sometimes arguably an improvement, notwithstanding the important goal of international standards. AIS target symbols are shown in Figure 3.12-1. Differences among ECS programs do occur in the cursor pick presentation of a selected AIS target, but the primary target data are always available. A sample is shown in Figure 3.12-2.

For those without an AIS receiver, some ECS programs offer an internet link to display nearly-live AIS for any part of the world. This is a very nice feature, but it is crucial to check the frequency of signals, presented in the display as the "time since last update." The legally prescribed update times we see with live AIS are listed in Table 3.12-1; they depend on vessel status and speed. They are 2 to 10 sec for Class A (commercial vessels) and 30 sec for Class B, which are primarily from recreational vessels. The "nearly-live" internet sources of AIS can be subject to delays of a few minutes, or even longer. The main value of these AIS signals is they show us locations of vessels at large distances off, but as they get closer to any level of collision risk, the signal delay could be dangerously misleading for even slow moving targets.

Some ECS programs offer AIS display with a built-in AIS DR option that reads the COG, SOG, and update time, and then shows a ghost icon of the AIS target in a DR mode moving away from the last reported position. This option

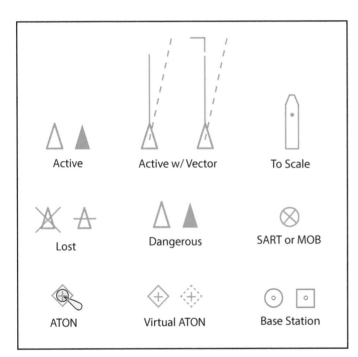

Figure 3.12-1. *Sample AIS target symbols shown on an ECS. Although standardized in ECDIS, there is variation in these basic icons seen in many ECS programs. Except for red on dangerous CPA and SART targets, colors and fill of the other symbols vary between ECS programs. User set options can turn on heading and COG predictors (dashed lines). The direction of turn can also be indicated. On large scale displays, an optional vector outline of the target vessel can be shown using dimensions broadcast. An ATON AIS target that is not on a charted symbol is a virtual ATON, meaning it marks a navigation reference point where there is no physical object at the location. Base stations are common targets seen, but rarely with navigational significance. They mark the hubs that keep the system working, and offer an ECS position check.*

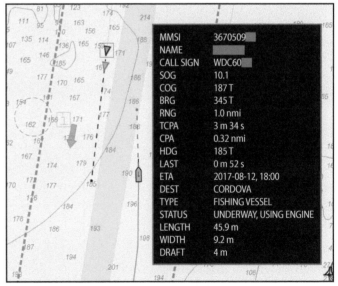

Figure 3.12-2. *Sample AIS target info display. Red target means its CPA is less than the user selected safe value. This one shows a ghost DR position since last AIS signal, which is valuable for Class B signals and all fast vessels, keeping in mind that even in best conditions some signals are missed. Destination and ETA are often out of date in these displays, if given at all.*

could mitigate reporting delays or missed signals, but must be interpreted very carefully.

There are two categories of data shown in each cursor pick report: static data that describe the vessel itself and voyage data that can include the destination and ETA. The static data (name, vessel type, numeric IDs, vessel dimensions, and more) are programmed into the AIS transceiver and will always be present, but the voyage data must be user entered and might be missing. The destinations can be in plain language (up to 20 characters) or in the 5-letter UN Code for Trade and Transportation Locations (UN/LOCODE).

AIS-transmitted dynamic data includes Lat, Lon, COG, SOG, and more, notably the vessel status, with options listed in Table 3.12-2. Most professional shipping will report vessel status properly, but not all. It is not uncommon to see a vessel moving down the waterway at 15 kts reporting a status of "At anchor," or to see a vessel clearly at anchor, showing "Underway using engine." This is a finable offense for the vessel, not just because safety is affected by wrong broadcast time-interval, but it also consumes bandwidth, which can put stress on the system in a busy harbor when there are many anchored vessels sending out signals too frequently (see Table 3.12-2).

Other types of AIS targets include AIS marked aids to navigation (ATON) such as buoys and bridge pylons, which in turn, raises awareness of the proximity of these to the same level as that of a radar RACON. *Virtual ATON* AIS targets mark key navigation locations on the waterway where there are no physical markers.

Having the name of each target vessel available to us via AIS data makes radio communications more effective, and the computed and displayed range and bearing to vessel AIS targets allows for numerical evaluation of closest point of approach (CPA) and the time to CPA (TCPA) with associated warning options.

Collision Avoidance with AIS Targets

We tend think of radar when discussing collision avoidance as it remains the primary electronic aid for evaluating collision risk. Nevertheless, AIS target display in an ECS can be a valuable aid for navigation in traffic, especially for vessels that do not have radar but have an ECS and AIS receiver.

Even with radar, AIS aids collision avoidance as it can reveal targets whose radar signals are blocked by islands or headlands or those obscured by heavy rain or snow. Also, AIS signals can be received in some cases from farther off than possible with a typical small-craft radar—AIS signals span about the same range as VHF radio reception.

Many small-craft radars do not have ARPA (automatic radar plotting aid)—or worse, they might have one that does not work properly due to faulty sensor calibration—so collision-risk evaluation with radar alone requires manually solving or interpreting the relative motion diagram. In contrast, AIS targets show computed, dynamic values of target COG and SOG (independent of any sensors on our vessel) with their actual tracks plotted out in true motion and real time on the chart. Thus the COG predictor lines of our vessel and those of the AIS targets provides a clear graphic picture of the interactions.

Essentially all ECS programs with AIS capability offer collision warning functions based on user input of a safe CPA and TCPA. An example is shown in Figure 3.12-3.

3.13 Navigational Warnings

Now we come to one of the main advantages of the ENCs over the RNCs. Namely, your ECS program knows where you are at all times from your GPS input, and when running an ENC, it also knows where everything else on the

Table 3.12-2. AIS Vessel Type and Status Options	
Vessel TYPE	*Vessel STATUS (Class A only)*
Not available	Underway using engine
Sailing vessel	At anchor
Pleasure craft	Not under command
Fishing vessel	Restricted maneuverability
Tug	Constrained by draft
Passenger ship	Moored
Cargo ship	Aground
Tanker	Engaged in fishing
Pilot vessel	Underway sailing
High-speed craft (HSC)	High-speed craft (HSC)
Wing in ground (WIG)	Wing in ground (WIG)
Law enforcement	Power-driven vessel towing astern
	Power-driven vessel pushing ahead or towing alongside
	AIS-SART

Table 3.12-1 AIS Class-A Compared to Class-B Features			
	Class A		*Class B*
Transmit Power (watt)	12.5W / 2W (low power)		2W*
Dynamic data reports	0 - 14 kt	10s	< 2 kt 3m
Underway**	14 - 23 kt	6s	> 2kt 30s
	>23 kt	2s	
Not underway	3m		3m
Static data reports	6m		6m
Voyage data reports	6m or when changed		——

* This low power implies for typical installations an effective range of 5 to 7 nmi, compared to 25 nmi or more for Class A.

** Class A reporting rate increased to 2 or 3 seconds when turning. Class B does not include rate of turn information.

chart is located at all times. Thus the ECS can use your COG and SOG to look ahead to see if you might be getting into any trouble, such as heading into water depths shallower than your safety contour, or hitting a rock or buoy, or any isolated danger. The functioning of your ECS with regard to the use of the warning potential of the ENC is an important feature to test early and throughly. It can also warn you of crossing other boundary lines on the chart.

This safety feature is unrelated to the AIS target warning; it addresses hazards and alerts of the waterway itself, not other traffic present. The AIS traffic display and warnings will work with RNCs or ENCs, but the navigational warnings require an ENC of the region be loaded. Many ECS programs, however, will let you set and use the navigational warnings when navigating on an RNC provided that you have an ENC of the same region loaded at the same time. With this approach, you navigate on what might be a more familiar RNC, while taking advantage of the digital information of the underlying ENC to provide the warnings. As noted in Section 2.10, there are several other good reasons for ECS users to have both RNCs and ENCs available.

You can set the warning time look-ahead to be the same or different from the displayed COG predictor time, depending on preference or circumstance, but in either case the use of a safety zone or anti-grounding cone look-ahead is more effective than just looking along the COG predictor line itself. The latter is just as effective for detecting the safety depth contour, but just looking along a straight line ahead could bring you closer to an isolated danger than you wanted. The safety zone option is required in type-approved ECDIS, but it is only implemented in some ECS programs. A sample is shown in Figure 3.13-3.

3.14 Simulator or Protected Waters Practice

Some of the tools and procedures outlined in this chapter can, to a large extent, be learned and mastered from an ECS located safely at home or at the dock, with no external connections. In a few cases, we can learn even more from a moving vessel icon in a DR mode, still safely at the kitchen table.

At some point, however, we need to study ECS functionality from a moving vessel, presumably in protected waters that let us experiment with frequent course and speed changes that do not endanger the navigation—or better still, practice with a realistic simulation of our own moving vessel that behaves just as if we were on the water driving our own vessel. Add simulated AIS traffic to this and we can expand the training even further.

Following is a list of ECS tools and skills that are learned more readily and thoroughly with a simulator, but it would be the same list to start with when practicing underway in protected waters. For this study and for the creation of several diagrams in this book, we used the Starpath eNav Trainer, a multi-vessel GPS, AIS, and VHF simulator listed in the References. It includes simulated wind and current.

Basic setup (Use ENC or RNC)

• If your ECS program offers both planning and navigation modes, then experiment with these during the exercises below to learn how they behave and how to switch between them.

• Set up digital display windows to watch HDG versus COG, STW versus SOG, cursor position versus GPS position as you get underway in your simulated vessel.

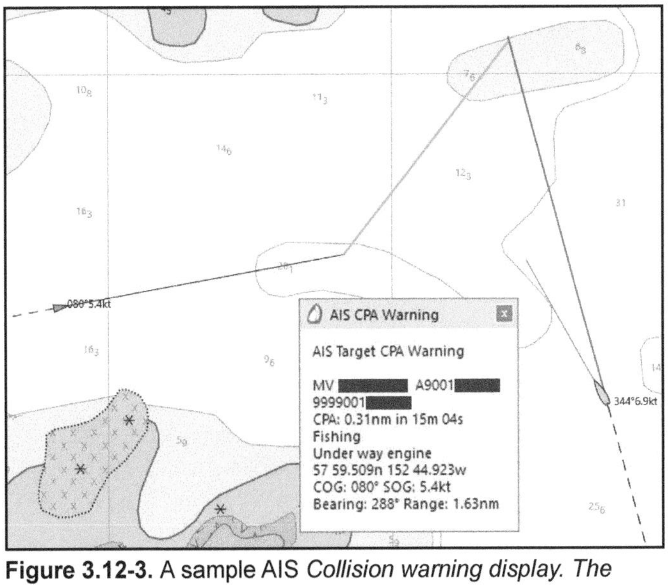

Figure 3.12-3. A sample AIS *Collision warning display. The dangerous AIS target is always changed to red, but otherwise these warning displays and associated options vary notably from one ECS to another.*

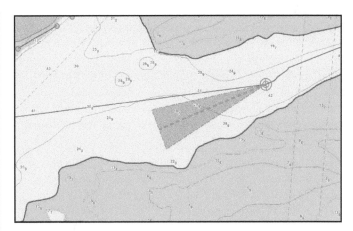

Figure 3.13-1. *Anti-grounding cone set at 20° angle and 6-min look ahead. This vessel will get an alarm if the cone touches the safety contour. This can be set to fixed time ahead or fixed distance ahead, both centered on the COG. The green line is the heading line, so we see this vessel is being set a lot by the local current.*

• Practice range and bearing measurements from your moving vessel.

• Turn on heading indicator and COG predictor, and practice varying their lengths. Then change speed significantly to see how these change. Use the measurement tool to confirm they are the lengths you expect.

• Vary the simulated current set and drift and vary your heading and speed to understand the data window displays.

• Check for sensor input averaging options in the ECS and practice how these affect your speed and course changes.

• Practice north-up, course-up, and head-up chart display while changing courses.

• Study "center on vessel" options, including when crossing chart boundaries.

• Check out the tracking options after several turns and how the settings affect what you see. Experiment with a high frequency and low frequency of tracking marks. In each case save the tracks and see how the tracks are stored.

• Drive around on a serpentine course and then save the track and convert it to a route, and then hide or delete the track and load the route to see what it looks like.

Basic Routes (no current, no wind)

In these exercises you can move your vessel with the simulator, or you can just move the route or its waypoints to set up the exercise more quickly.

• Practice route navigation to a single waypoint (WP) from present vessel position, sometimes called "navigate to point," or you just place a point and activate it. (Activating a WP makes it the target of the navigation.) Use digital display windows to show: distance to waypoint (DWP), bearing to waypoint (BWP), speed made good to WP (VMC), and cross track error (XTE). Also show the name of the next WP. Watch these values as you turn and head to the WP. Then once on a steady course toward the WP, turn off course and watch these parameters change. *Note there are not standard abbreviations for these parameters; we use the ones above for convenience only.*

• Practice getting into a pre-defined route. Create a 2-leg route from a WP1 to a WP2, due north of it, followed by large turn to a WP3. Position your vessel some distance southwest of WP1. The goal is to get onto leg1 (WP1 to WP2) with WP2 activated.

Look for different behaviors between "activate WP" and "activate route." See how this varies depending on where you are relative to WP1. If you are well north of WP1 and quite a ways west of leg 1, the program will try to take you directly to WP2, which covers waters well off of the leg 1 line, which are hypothetically dangerous. Practice ways to get onto leg 1 with WP2 activated in the most direct manner.

• Practice activating routes, then deactivating, then activate a WP, then the route, and various combinations to see that all works as intended.

• Then start over again headed to WP2, and study the options for advancing to WP3 as the active waypoint, once you reach WP2. There are manual and automatic options.

Check the properties of WP2 to set an arrival range ring. Practice driving to WP2 along the course line to see how this behaves. Watch the name of next waypoint display. Are there any alarms that can be set? Then try a larger arrival range than seems necessary to see if might recommend a turn too early. Some autopilots can be set to turn the vessel automatically, so it is crucial to understand this process when using them.

Then try a very small arrival range and consider the risk of missing the turn altogether. We will not necessarily be on course as we approach the waypoint.

Routes with Current (need simulated current)

• Now add a knot or two of current across the route, and do these exercises again. Watch your track and digital displays. Practice steering to hold the course line on leg 1 and then on leg 2. These are valuable exercises for those who sail in strong current.

• Head off on some course across the current, and practice the methods of Section 3.11 on determining the set and drift and compare with the simulated values.

Alarms and alerts (need ENC charts)

• Check alerts setup parameters in your ECS. Check safety depth and safety contour settings. Is there a depth contour in the ENC that matches your chosen safety depth?— if not, the ECS will select the next deepest contour. Check when an alarm should go off. The possibilities are: when the vessel icon reaches the hazard; when the leading edge of the COG predictor reaches the hazard; or at a separate user defined distance or time ahead.

Then head into the beach to see when the alarm goes off. What happens if the safety contour is different from the safety depth? Do the same headed directly toward any rock or isolated danger.

• Then choose a safety depth shallower the nearest safety contour and try again to look for differences. That is, does the alarm occur at safety depth or safety contour. Note some ECS programs may not use those terms and instead let you enter a depth specifically for the alert.

• Do the following without an anti-grounding or safety zone, using only the COG predictor line to detect the hazard. Find an isolated danger symbol and use it for the target to check the warnings again by driving straight toward it, noting carefully if it is the safety depth or safety contour that signals the alarm. In an ECS with user set alarm depths, test to see how these behave with underwater rocks of known depths. Generally in ECS programs, and according to ECDIS standards, the tide height should not be taken into account in these alerts.

• With an anti-grounding or safety zone available, turn it on and do the above again, and confirm that the alarm is triggered when your safety zone touches or approaches the hazard.

• ECS alarms might also work for crossing certain charted boundary lines, but not many meet ECDIS standards on this, possibly because there are so many such lines on an ENC it could be distracting. Check the ECS to see how this is covered and test it. If the ECS does not recognize the ENC boundary data, it will likely still go off crossing a custom boundary you define. Check this, which should work with RNCs as well as ENCs.

AIS collision avoidance alarms (requires simulated or live AIS traffic)

• The key here is getting access to moving AIS traffic in your ECS. This can be live from your own receiver or from an internet source or it could be simulated AIS traffic. The DR mode of your ECS might also interact with AIS traffic without simulated GPS signals.

• Practice setting CPA and TCPA limits, and see how the alerts are presented. Some have audio or graphic, some have both. Some draw in various vectors on the chart between your vessel icon and the target; others do not. In all cases a dangerous target icon should change to red.

• Check out the various digital target lists, and options for showing these; check and test settings for target filters, or behavior when target signals are lost.

• There are always extensive lists of options for viewing AIS targets, and they vary with ECS brand. There is much to practice with for this extremely important tool.

Wind data display (need simulated anemometer)

• A simulated wind sensor provides apparent wind angle (AWA) and apparent wind speed (AWS), assuming a constant user selected true wind speed (TWS) and true wind direction (TWD). Set up display windows to show AWA, AWS, TWS, TWD, and true wind angle (TWA).

• With no current, head into the wind and stop. In this case the true wind and apparent wind should be identical. Turn 30° to the right of the wind and stop, read the dials, and then 30° to the left of the wind, stop, and read the dials. Then carry on around in either direction, always stopping, to check the wind and watch how the displays switch from port to starboard side winds.

• Then face into the wind at AWA about 50°, stop, read the dials, then maintaining that heading, start to increase the speed. You should see AWA move forward, AWS increase, but TWA, TWS, and TWD should remain the same.

• Carry out the same exercise headed downwind, at say 150° AWA.

3.15 Route Optimization in ECS programs

Section 3.11 discussed displaying tidal currents in ECS programs as both plain graphic arrows for manual routing and in digital format that can then be incorporated into optimum routing computations. Racing sailors are accustomed to doing their own weather routing using GRIB formatted wind, current, and sea state forecasts. The same type of analysis is used by many global shipping companies to save time, fuel, and enhance cargo protection. Obviously the performance parameters that enter into the process are quite different in these two cases, and the ship routing is generally done from a land based contractor and not from the vessel itself as on sailing vessels.

The main point here is that ECS is not just a more efficient approach to traditional chart navigation, it is a powerful tool for selecting the optimum route in varying conditions. This can be done by loading the environmental data into the ECS—it is available by email request—and manually stepping forward in time to see how conditions vary along optional routes. This is possible with almost any ECS these days, but selected ECS programs go further by including route optimization routines that use this data and the known performance characteristics of the vessel to then numerically propose the best route under various assumptions.

This type of weather routing, however, is never "plug and play"; it takes practice to obtain truly optimum routes, and it requires accurate performance data that can indeed be met in the conditions at hand. For sailing vessels this takes the form of accurate polar diagrams and knowledge of how these are affected by sea state. Shipping companies rely on similar data on how specific ships with specific loading respond to wind and waves at various angles and intensities. With that said, even without the best performance data, or without the most sophisticated analysis program, we can often learn crucial matters of route selection over long routes that we might have missed without these tools.

Furthermore, even though individually we might not have access to the state of the art analysis program, nor the best possible performance data for our vessel, we all still have access to essentially the same environmental data as those with the best possible analysis tools. Global ocean wind, current, and sea state data are readily available, as are high resolution inland and coastal wind data in many locations. Ocean current data are generally less reliable than wind data on a global basis, but the data are readily available to all mariners. Part of the "not plug and play" aspect is that we must train ourselves to best evaluate the data that go into the routing. Figures 3.15-1 to 3.15-3 show examples of Ocean data that can be loaded into an ECS to assist in route planning.

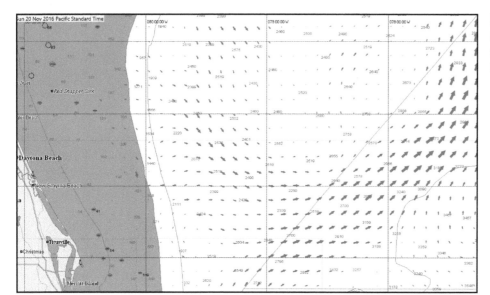

Figure 3.15-1. *Gulf Stream currents as a GRIB file that can be used in route optimization. This is HYCOM ocean model.*

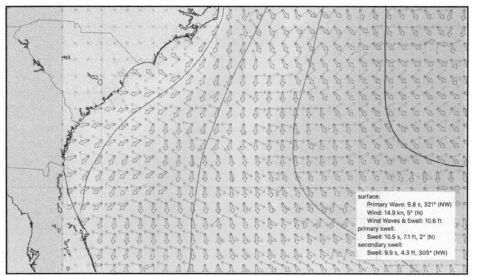

Figure 3.15-2. *Detailed sea state forecasts are available every 6 hours in GRIB format from the NWS WW3 model.*

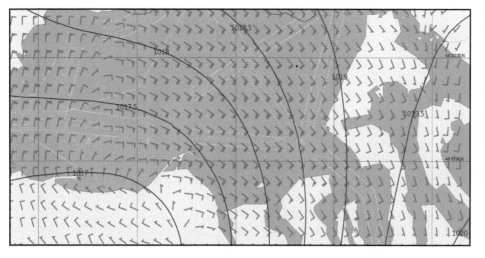

Figure 3.15-3. *Wind data in GRIB format overlaid in an ECS. These data can in turn be used for computed optimal weather routing of sailing vessels. This example is from the High Resolution Rapid Refresh model (HRRR), which is updated hourly and extends out 18 hours. This is the most accurate U.S. wind forecast for this 18-hr time period; it has a resolution of 3 km (1.6 nmi).*

Chapter 4

Annotated ECDIS Chart No. 1

Introduction

This chapter of the book is essentially a reproduction of the ECDIS part of *U.S. Chart No. 1*, which we have abbreviated in some cases and reformatted. We have then added annotations to clarify some symbols and provided cross references to sections in the text where appropriate. To distinguish what we have added from the original text of *U.S. Chart No. 1*, our annotations appear in *[square brackets, using blue italic font]*.

Columns in the body of the Chapter have this format:

Category and symbol	Short description	Paper Chart Equivalent
◉	Land as a point at small scale	K 10
◉ 8 m	Land as an area, with an elevation or control point	K 10
✳	Rock which covers and uncovers or is awash at low water	K 11, K 12

The paper chart equivalents refer to the International Symbols (INT 1) listed in *U.S. Chart No. 1*. When there are multiple references given it means the ECDIS symbol has multiple meanings, as many do. As stressed throughout, a cursor pick is the key to learning the meaning of individual symbols, lines, and areas. Click everything! The main reference for our annotations is IHO S-52 Presentation Library, version 3.4, with awareness of proposed changes in version 4.0 planned to be in effect Sept 1, 2017.

ECDIS Color Palettes

ECDIS allows the mariner to change the color palette that is used to display an ENC. Three different color tables have been designed to provide the maximum clarity and contrast between features on the display under three different lighting conditions on the bridge, namely Day, Dusk and Night.

Each symbol is rendered in a different color appropriate for the lighting condition that the color table is meant for. This design provides maximum contrast for the display on a sunny day, as well as preserving night vision on a dimly lit bridge in the evening. This allows the mariner to look back and forth between the chart on the ECDIS display and out to sea through the bridge window without the mariner's eyes needing to readjust to a difference in light intensity.

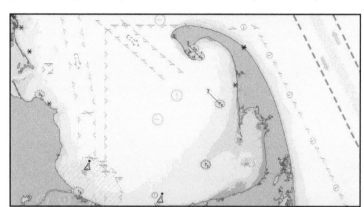

The Day Color Table, meant to be used in bright sunlight, uses a white background for deep water and looks the most like a traditional paper chart.

[This book only uses the daytime color palette.]

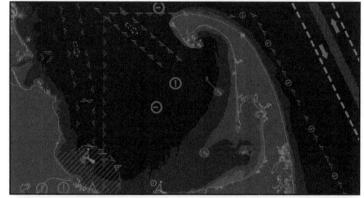

The Dusk Color Table uses a black background for deep water and colors are subdued, but slightly brighter than those used in the Night Color Table.

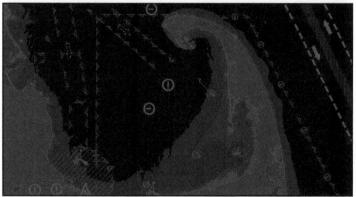

The Night Color Table, meant to be used in the darkest conditions, uses a black background for deep water and muted color shades for other features.

[These three ENC color palettes are similar to those used in RNCs, which are listed digitally in the header to the RNC's KAP file. The daytime palette is intended to emulate printed charts, but with print-on-demand, print palettes can be adjusted by individual producers, which can lead to improvements that do not precisely match the original NOAA lithographic standards. Also, the final print palettes can vary with the paper stock, which is an option from some producers. Furthermore, although the PDF version of U.S. Chart No. 1 should display the intended colors, once it has been printed by a third party for personal use or commercial distribution (including this book), we are susceptible to the uncertainties of the printing process, which can lead to color differences between products.]

A. Mariners' Navigational Symbols

[Section A is not part of the U.S. Chart No. 1. These displays are determined by the ECS or ECDIS program. They are similar for all ECDIS, but differ notably among ECS programs.]

AIS *[See Section 3.12.]*		
△ △ ▲	Sleeping AIS target	
△ △ ▲	Active AIS target	
△ △ ▲	Dangerous AIS target	
✕	Lost AIS target	
⌐	AIS target turning to starboard	
¬	AIS target turning to port	
⟡⊕	AIS based aid to navigation	
⬙	AIS target, true scale outline	
⊗	AIS SART (Search and Rescue Transmitter) symbol	
⊙	AIS base station	

Examples of AIS Course Over Ground (COG), and Speed Over Ground (SOG) vector and targets
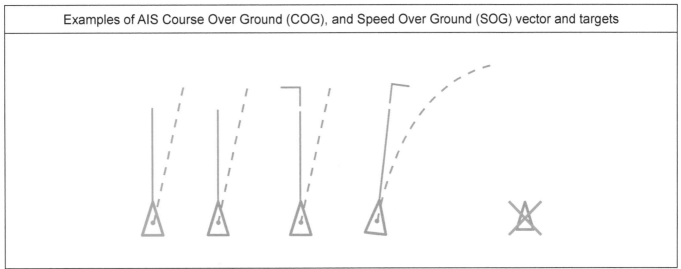

Route Information *[See Section 3.2-3.4.]*			
—	Time mark on past track		
—	Time mark on secondary past track		
⬭	Surrounding ellipse for arrival date and time at planned position		
—	Cross line for planned position		
▭	Box for speed to make good, planned route *[red]*		
▭	Box for speed to make good, alternate route *[orange]*		
◯	Waypoint on planned route *[red]*		
◯	Waypoint on alternate planned route *[orange]*		
◎	Next waypoint on planned route		
• • • • • • • • • • • • •	Planned route for own ship		

Example of route and waypoints	Example of past tracks
16/1235 10 Next waypoint Waypoint Alternate route	▬▬▬▬▬▬ ▬▬▬▬▬▬

Manual Update Information			
╱	This object or line has been manually deleted or modified		
╎	This object has been manually updated		
◯	This line has been manually updated		

	Examples of manual updates	
	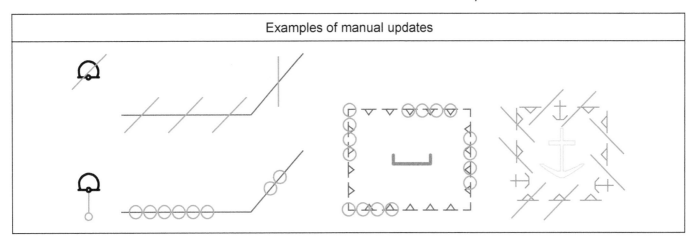	

Chart Display Information		
$+$	Ordinary cursor	
$+$	Cursor with open center	
N↑	North arrow	
$\#$	Reference point, "ghost cursor" (user interface)	
▌	One mile scale bar for display scales larger than 1:80,000 *[mile = nautical mile]* *[See Section 2.3.]*	
▌	10 mile latitude scale for display scales smaller than 1:80,000 *[mile = nautical mile]*	

	Chart scale boundary, the double line indicates the larger scale	
	Overscale pattern *[Many ECS do not use this symbol.]*	

Chart Tools

	Arrowhead for mariners clearing line *[Danger Bearing]*	
	Point of origin for an offset Electronic Bearing Line (EBL) or Variable Range Marker (VRM)	
	Range mark for an Electronic Range and Bearing Line (ERBL)	

Example of EBL and VRM offset, and own ship ERBL	Example of Clearing Line *[Danger Bearing]*
	NLT 040 deg

	Electronic Range and Bearing Line	
	Own ship position fix	

Radar Information			
⊙		Automatic Radar Plotting Aid (ARPA) target	
—		One minute mark on an ARPA vector	
—		Six minute mark on an ARPA vector	
⟪		Arrowhead for ARPA (or AIS) vector course and speed over ground	
⌃		Arrowhead for ARPA (or AIS) vector course and speed through the water	

Example of ARPA water vector
⊙-�-franco⟩

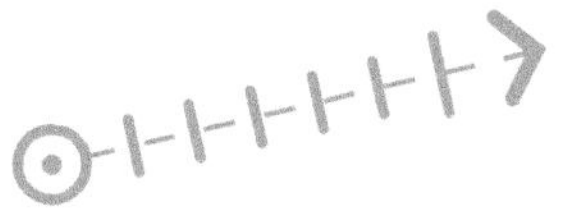

Annotations			
	i	Mariners' information note	
	⊙	Mariners' caution note	
	▧	Mariners' event mark	
	i	Manufacturer's information note	
	⊙	Manufacturer's caution note	
▢	⊕	Transparent danger highlight for mariners' use	
	↑↑↑	Predicted tidal stream or current direction	
	↟↟	Actual tidal stream or current direction	
▭	P 3.2 ↑↑↑	Box for current strength	

Own Ship Information *[See Section 3.7.]*		
—	One minute mark for own ship vector	
—	Six minute mark for own ship vector	
◎	Own ship symbol, constant size	
⬭	Own ship drawn to scale with conning position marked	
⋀⋀	Arrowhead for own ship vector course and speed over ground	
⋀	Arrowhead for own ship vector course and speed through the water	

Examples of Course Over Ground (COG), Speed Over Ground (SOG) vector, safety frame/anti-grounding cone.
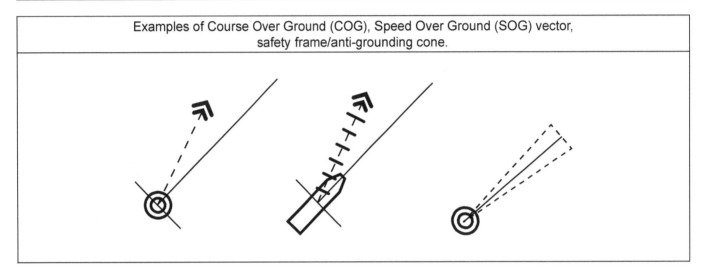

B. Positions, Distances, Directions, Compass

Geographical Positions		
PA	Position approximate	B 7
?	Point feature or area of low accuracy	B 7, B 8
(21)	Sounding of low accuracy	B 7, B 8

Control Points		
o	Position of an elevation or control point	B 20-24
km 7	Canal and distance point with no mark *[Unmarked distance point along a canal.]*	B 25.1
∘km 7	Canal and distance point *[Visible distance mark along a canal.]*	B 25.2

Note: ECDIS uses a magenta "km" symbol to represent distance marks. However, the distances shown along waterways on NOAA-produced ENCs are displayed in statute miles. [Rivers, Great Lakes, Intracoastal]

Symbolized Positions (Examples)		
ECDIS follows the paper chart convention for the position of symbols, except for simplified symbols for buoys and beacons (see Q 1).		B 30, B 31
⊙	Position of a point feature *[Brown when non-conspicuous.]*	B 32
ECDIS indicates approximate position only for wrecks, obstructions, islets and shoreline features.		B 33

Magnetic Compass *[See Section 2.13.]*		
Varn	Magnetic Variation	B 60
◀	Cursor pick site for magnetic variation at a point	B 68.1, B70

	Cursor pick site for magnetic variation over an area	B 68.1
Varn - 3	Cursor pick site for magnetic variation along a line *[Example shown is 3° West. West is negative; East is positive.]*	B 71
	Cursor pick site for magnetic anomaly along a line or over an area	B 82.1, B 82.2

C. Natural Features

Coastline *[See Section 2.10.]*

	Coastline *[Nature of coastline (cliffs, etc.) is obtained by cursor pick.]*	C 1
	Coastline or shoreline construction of low accuracy in position *[Does not show if accuracy not encoded.]*	C 2
	Sloping ground crest line distant from coastline, radar or visually conspicuous	C 3
	Cliff as an area *[There are more cliff symbols in RNC than ENC.]*	C 3
	Conspicuous hill or mountain top *[Brown when non-conspicuous.]*	C 4, C 8

Relief [*See Section 2.10*]		
	Elevation contour with spot height, contour value is obtained by cursor pick [*Many ENCs do not show elevation contours that are depicted on the corresponding RNCs.*]	C 10, C 12-13
	Position of an elevation or control point	C 11
Water Features, Lava		
	River	C 20, C 21
	Rapids Waterfall Waterfall, visually conspicuous	C 22
	Lake [*See Section 2.10.*]	C 23
	Continuous pattern for an ice area (glacier, etc.)	C 25
Vegetation [*See Section 2.6, 2.10.*]		
	Line of trees	C 30, C 31.2, C 31.3
	Wooded area	C 30, C 31.5-8
	Tree [*Height of a tree is sometimes available via cursor pick.*]	C 31.1, C 31.2

	Mangrove with coastline or shoreline construction of low accuracy in position	C 32
	Marsh with coastline or shoreline construction of low accuracy in position	C 33

D. Cultural Features

Settlements, Buildings *[See Section 2.10.]*

	Built-up area	D 1
	Built-up area as a point	D 3, D 4
	Conspicuous single building *[Brown border when non-conspicuous.]*	D 5
	Conspicuous single building in built-up area	D 6
	Street names and status of ruins can be obtained by cursor pick	D 7, D 8

Roads, Railways, Airfields *[See Section 2.10.]*

	Road, track or path as a line	D 10-12
	Road as an area	D 10-12
	Railway, with station	D 13
	Cutting	D 14
	Embankment	D 15

	Embankment, visually or radar conspicuous	D 15
	Tunnel	D 16
	Tunnel with depth below the seabed encoded	D 16
	Airport as a point	D 17
	Runway as a line	D 17
	Airport area, with runway area and visually conspicuous runway area	D 17
clr 20.0 clr cl 20.0 clr op 20.0 sf clr 20.0	Vertical clearance Closed clearance Open clearance Safe clearance	D 20
clr 20.0 clr 20.0	Bridge	D 22, D 23.5, D 24
clr cl 8.2 clr op 20.0 clr cl 8.2 clr op 20.0	Opening bridge	D 23.1-4, D 23.6
clr 20.0	Aerial or overhead cableway	D 25, D 27
clr 20.0	Aerial or overhead cableway, radar conspicuous	D 25, D 27
sf clr 20.0	Transmission line	D 26
sf clr 20.0	Transmission line, radar conspicuous	D 26
clr 20.0	Overhead pipeline	D 28
clr 20.0	Overhead pipeline, radar conspicuous	D 28
	Oil, gas pipeline, submerged or on land	D 29

ECDIS Conspicuous and Non-Conspicuous Features

There are 25 features for which ECDIS displays either a black symbol, if the feature is visually conspicuous, or a brown symbol if is not. Only conspicuous landmarks are depicted on NOAA paper charts and ENCs. Therefore, only the conspicuous symbol versions are shown in the symbol tables of U.S. Chart No. 1. Both versions of the symbols for these features are shown on this page. *[These colors are sometimes difficult to distinguish, depending on the ECS.]*

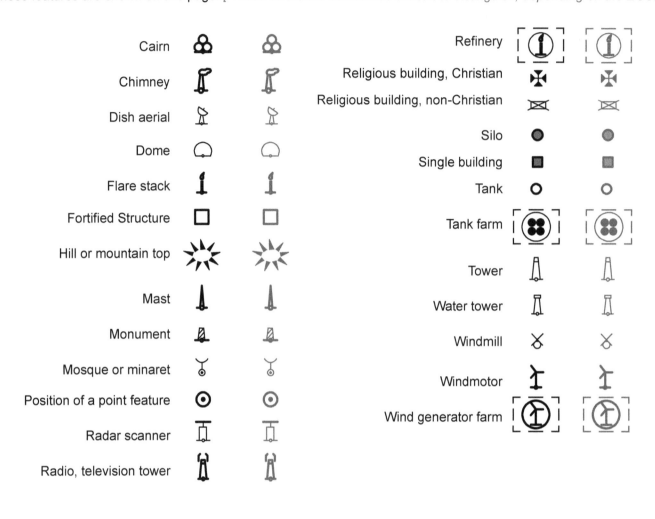

These seven symbols represent features that only have a brown symbol. There is no corresponding black, conspicuous symbol. The brown symbol is displayed regardless of the conspicuousness of the feature.

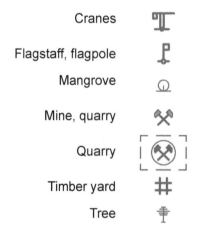

E. Landmarks

[Height above ground level and/or above height datum is obtained by cursor pick.]

General		
⊙	Non-conspicuous point feature	E 1
▪	Non-conspicuous building	E 1
🝙	Non-conspicuous water tower	E 1
⊙	Conspicuous point feature	E 2, E 12
▪	Conspicuous building	E 2
🝙	Conspicuous water tower	E 2
🝙 i	The information symbol is displayed if a supplemental image is available, which may be accessed by cursor pick *[NOAA ENCs do not include images, but in principle they could be added by the user.]*	E 3.1

Landmarks		
✠	Church as a point, church tower, spire, dome, or chapel	E 10.1, E 10.2-4, E 11
⬦	Church as an area	E 10.1
⋈	Religious building, non-Christian	E 13-16
⚲	Mosque or minaret	E 17, E18
▭	Landmark area	E 19
🝙	Tower, radar tower	E 20
🝙	Water tower	E 21
🝙	Chimney	E 22
🕯	Flare stack	E 23
🝙	Monument	E 24

	Windmill	E 25.1, E 25.2
	Wind motor	E 26.1
	Wind generator farm	E 26.2
	Flagstaff, flagpole	E 27
	Mast	E 28, E 30.1
	Radio, television tower	E 29
	Radar scanner	E 30.3
	Dome	E 30.4
	Dish aerial	E 31
	Tank	E 32
	Tank farm	E 32
	Silo	E 33
	Fortified structure	E 34.1
	Fortified structure	E 34.2, E 34.3
	Quarry area	E 35.1
	Quarry	E 35.2

F. Ports

	Protective Structures	
	Dike as a line	F 1
	Dike as a line, conspicuous	F 1
	Dike as an area	F 1
	Seawall	F 2.1, F 2.2
	Causeway as a line	F 3
	Causeway, covers and uncovers as a line	F 3
	Causeway as an area	F 3
	Causeway, covers and uncovers as an area	F 3
	Breakwater or mole as a line	F 4.1-3, F 12
	Breakwater or mole as an area	F 4.1-3, F 12
	Training wall	F 5
	Groin (always dry)	F 6.1
	Groin (intertidal)	F 6.2
	Groin (submerged)	F 6.3

	Harbor Installations *[See Section 1.7.]*	
	Fishing harbor	F 10
	Yacht harbor, marina	F 11.1, F 19.2
	Wharf (quay)	F 13

	Pier (jetty), promenade pier	F 14, F 15
	Pontoon as a line	F 16
	Pontoon as an area	F16
	Landing	F 17
	Landing steps	F 18
	Berth number	F 19.1
	Mooring dolphin	F 20
	Deviation mooring dolphin	F 21
	Pile or bollard	F 22
	Slipway, ramp	F 23
	Gridiron	F 24
	Dry dock	F 25
	Floating dock as line	F 26
	Floating dock as an area	F 26
	Wet dock and gate	F 27
	Dock	F 28
	Dock, under construction or ruined	F 28

	Floating hazard	F 29.1
	Boom	F 29.1
	Floating oil barrier, oil retention (high pressure pipe)	F 29.1, F 29.2
	Boom, floating obstruction	F 29.1
	Ruin or works under construction Year and condition of under construction or ruin is obtained by cursor pick	F 30-33.1
	Pier, ruined and partly submerged	F 33.2
	Hulk	F 34
Canals, Barrages		
	Canal	F 40
	Lock gate as a line	F 41.1
	Lock gate as an area	F 41.1
	Navigable lock gate	F 41.2
	Non-navigable lock gate	F 42, F 43
	Caisson as a line	F 42
	Caisson as an area	F 42
	Flood barrage as a line	F 43
	Flood barrage as an area	F 43

	Dam as a line	F 44
	Dam as an area	F 44
Transhipment Facilities		
RoRo	RoRo Terminal	F 50
#	Timber yard as a point	F 52
#	Timber yard as an area	F 52
⊥	Crane as a point, lifting capacity is obtained by cursor pick	F 53.1-3
	Crane as an area	F 53.1-3
	Crane, visually conspicuous as an area	F 53.1-3
Public Buildings		
⊖	Customs	F 61
▪	*[On ENCs, public buildings (harbormaster, hospital, post office, etc.) are shown as regular buildings.]*	F 60-63

H. Tides, Currents

	Tide Tables		
◇		Point or area for which a tidal stream table is available *[Actual data not included in U.S. or Canadian ENCs.]*	H 31, H 46
		Boundary of an area for which there is tidal information	H 31, H 40, H 41

	Tidal Streams and Currents		
2.5 kn		Flood stream, rate at spring tides *[Spring currents are about 20% stronger than average.]*	H 40
? ?		Current or tidal stream whose direction is not known	H 40, H 41
2.5 kn		Ebb stream, rate at spring tides	H 41
2.5 kn		Non-tidal current	H 42, H 43
		Overfalls, tide rips; eddies; breakers as point *[Cursor pick for important distinctions.]*	H 44, H 45
		Overfalls, tide rips; eddies; breakers as a line	H 44, H 45
		Overfalls, tide rips; eddies; breakers as an area	H 44, H 45

I. Depths

[ENC base units are meters, so U.S. charts with native units of feet and fathoms have soundings and depth contours encoded with decimal meters, expressed as subscripts.]

General		
(25)	Sounding of low accuracy	I 1, I 2, I 3.1, I 4
(212)	Underwater hazard with depth greater than 20 meters	I 2, I 4
⊗	Isolated danger of depth less than the safety contour	I 2, I 4
?	Point feature or area of low accuracy	I 3.1, I4
□ □ □ □ □	Low accuracy line demarking area wreck or obstruction	I 3.2
□ □ □ □ □	Low accuracy line demarking foul area	I 3.2
⊙	Obstruction, depth not stated	I 4
(5)	Underwater hazard with depth of 20 meters or less	I 4
Soundings *[See Section 2.4.]*		
9_7	Sounding shoaler than or equal to safety depth	I 10
30	Sounding deeper than safety depth	I 10
Depths are always shown in their true position in ECDIS		I 11, I 12
(12)	Sounding of low accuracy	I 14
4	Drying height, less than or equal to safety depth	I 15
	Tideway	I 16

Depths in Fairways and Areas [*See Section 2.11.*]

	Dredged area Depth, date of latest survey and other information is obtained by cursor pick [*Often shown in named parallel strips.*]	I 20-23
swept to 9.6	Swept area	I 24
	Incompletely surveyed area	I 25
	Unsurveyed area	I 25

ECDIS Portrayal of Depths

ECDIS depth related symbols closely resemble their paper chart counterparts; however, ECDIS provides valuable additional information to mariners that paper charts cannot.

Soundings
ECDIS enables mariners to set their own-ship "safety depth." If no depth is set, ECDIS sets the value to 30m. Soundings equal to or shoaler than the safety depth are shown in black; deeper soundings are displayed in a less conspicuous gray. Fractional values are shown with subscript numbers of the same size.

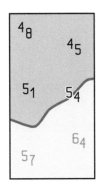

Depth Contours & Depth Areas
Depth contours in ECDIS are portrayed with a thin gray line. Each pair of adjacent depth contours is used to create depth area features. These are used by ECDIS to tint different depth levels and to initiate alarms when a ship is headed into unsafe water. [*A 5.4 m (17.7 ft) contour on a NOAA ENC corresponds to the 18 ft contour on the parent RNC. See Section 2.4.*]

Depth Contour Labels
ECDIS depth contour labels are not centered and oriented along isolines as they appear on paper charts. They are displayed upright and may appear either on or next to the contour lines that they describe. The labels are black and the same size as soundings, but the labels have a light "halo" to set them apart. The graphic to the left shows depth labels and soundings both deeper and shoaler than the safety depth. Note that depths on NOAA paper charts and ENCs are usually compiled in

fathoms and feet. Because ECDIS displays depths in meters, soundings and contour lines often show fractional meter values. The "own-ship safety contour" (described below) is always displayed, but mariners may choose to have all other depth contours turned off.

Safety Contour

ECDIS uses a "safety contour" value to show an extra thick line for the depth contour that separates "safe water" from shoaler areas. If the mariner does not set an own-ship safety contour value, ECDIS sets the value to 30m. If the ENC being displayed does not have a contour line equal to the safety contour depth value set by the mariner, then ECDIS sets the next deeper contour as the safety contour. Depending on the contour intervals used on individual ENCs, ECDIS may set different safety contours as a ship transits from one ENC to another. ECDIS will initiate an alarm if the ship's future track will cross the safety contour within a specified time set by the mariner.

Two or Four Tints for Shading Depth Areas

ECDIS tints all depth areas beyond the (green tinted) foreshore in either one of two or one of four shades of blue. This is similar to the convention used for paper charts, but the depths used to change from one tint to another are based on the safety contour and thus "customized" for each ship. If the mariner chooses two shades to be displayed, water deeper than the safety contour is shown in an off-white color, water shoaler than the safety contour is tinted blue.

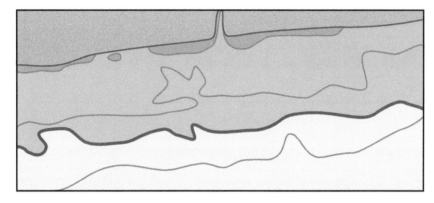

Portrayal of Depth Areas with 2 Color Settings

Some ECDIS enable mariners to define two additional depth areas for medium-deep water and medium-shallow water by setting a "deep contour" value and a "shallow contour" value. If this option is used, the safety contour is displayed between the medium deep and medium shallow contours.

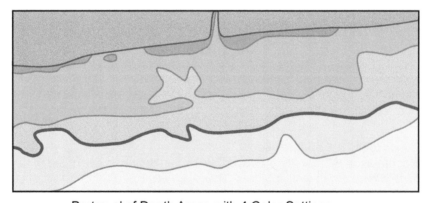

Portrayal of Depth Areas with 4 Color Settings

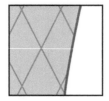
Some ECDIS also provide the mariner with the option of displaying a cross-hatch "shallow water" pattern over all depth areas shoaler than the safety contour.

Depth Contours *[See Section 2.4.]*

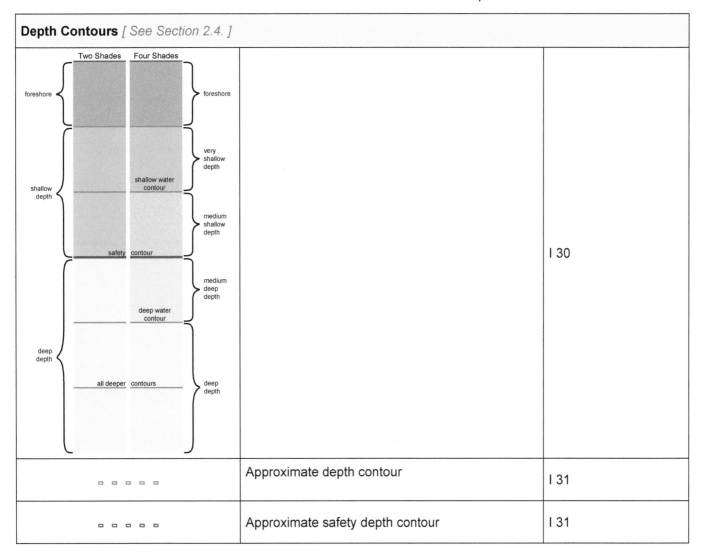

		I 30
▫ ▫ ▫ ▫ ▫	Approximate depth contour	I 31
▫ ▫ ▫ ▫ ▫	Approximate safety depth contour	I 31

J. Nature of the Seabed

Types of Seabed

S	Sand *[0.06 mm to 2 mm]*	J 1
M	Mud	J 2
Cy	Clay	J 3
Si	Silt	J 4
St	Stones	J 5
G	Gravel *[2 mm to 4 mm (buckshot to marbles)]*	J 6
P	Pebbles *[4 mm to 64 mm (marbles to golf balls)]*	J 7
Cb	Cobbles *[64 mm to 256 mm (golf balls to soccer balls)]*	J 8
R	Rock	J 9.1
R	Boulder *[bigger than cobbles]*	J 9.2
R	Lava	J 9.2
Co	Coral	J 10
Sh	Shells	J 11
	Weed, kelp	J 13.1
	Weed, kelp as an area	J 13.2
	Sand waves as a point	J 14
	Sand waves as a line	J 14
	Sand waves as an area	J 14
	Spring	J 15

Types of Seabed, Intertidal Areas

gravel / stone	Areas of gravel and stone *[See Types of Seabed.]*	J 20
	Rocky ledges or coral reef	J 21, J 22

K. Rocks, Wrecks, Obstructions, Aquaculture

[Key attributes of rocks and wrecks and obstructions are: water level effect and value of sounding.]

General *[See Section 2.5.]*

	Obstruction, depth not stated	K 1, K 16, K 40, K 43
	Obstruction which covers and uncovers	K 1
5	Underwater hazard with depth of 20 meters or less	K 1, K 14, K 26, K 41, K 43, K 46.1
⊗	Isolated danger of depth less than the safety contour *[This is activated by safety contour, not safety depth.]*	K 1, K 11, K 12-14, K 16, K 26-28, K 30, K 40-43, K 46
	Foul area, not safe for navigation	K 1
4	Swept sounding, less than or equal to safety depth	K 2
21	Swept sounding, greater than safety depth	K 2

Rocks *[See Section 2.6.]*

	Land as a point at small scale	K 10
8 m	Land as an area, with an elevation or control point	K 10
✳	Rock which covers and uncovers or is awash at low water	K 11, K 12
4	Underwater hazard which covers and uncovers with drying height	K 11, K 12
	Underwater hazard which covers and uncovers	K 12
⊕	Dangerous underwater rock of uncertain depth	K 13, K 16
25	Underwater hazard with depth greater than 20 meters	K 14, K 15, K 26, K 30, K 41, K 46.2
10	Underwater hazard with a depth of 20 meters or less	K 15,
⊗	Safe clearance shoaler than safety contour***	K 16, K 40, K 46.1, K 46.2
12₈	Safe clearance deeper than safety contour	K 16
(25₆)	Safe clearance deeper than 20 meters	K 16, K 46.2
	Overfalls, tide rips; eddies; breakwaters as a point	K 17
	Overfalls, tide rips; eddies; breakwaters as a line	K 17

	Overfalls, tide rips; eddies; breakwaters as an rea	K 17
Wrecks and Fouls		
	Wreck, always dry, with height shown	K 20
	Wreck, covers and uncovers	K 21
	Distributed remains of wreck	K 21
	Submerged wreck with depth of 20 meters or less	K 22
	Submerged wreck with depth greater than 20 meters	K 22
	Distributed remains of wreck	K 22
	Submerged wreck with depth less than the safety contour or depth unknown	K 23
	Wreck showing any portion of hull or superstructure at level of chart datum	K 24, K 25
	Swept sounding for underwater hazard less than safety depth	K 27
	Swept sounding for underwater hazard greater than or equal to safety depth	K 27
	Dangerous wreck, depth unknown	K 28
	Non-dangerous wreck, depth unknown	K 29
#	Foul area of seabed safe for navigation but not for anchoring	K 31.1, K 31.2
	Foul ground	K 31.1, K 31.2
	Distributed remains of wreck	K 31.1, K 31.2

4 (swept depth) 21 (swept depth) 5 (known by diver or other means) 25 (known by diver or other means)	Less than or equal to safety depth Greater than safety depth Underwater hazard with depth of 20 meters or less Underwater hazard with depth greater than 20 meters	K 42
Fish stakes symbol	Fish stakes as a point	K 44.1
Fish stakes area symbol	Fish stakes as an area	K 44.1
Fish trap point symbol	Fish trap, fish weir, tunny net as a point	K 44.2
Fish trap area symbol	Fish trap, fish weir, tunny net as an area	K 45
Marine farm point symbol	Marine farm as a point	K 47
Marine farm area symbol	Marine farm as an area	K 48.1, K 48.2

L. Offshore Installations

General

Symbol	Area where entry is prohibited or restricted or to be avoided, with other cautions	L 3
Symbol	Cautionary area, navigate with caution Wind farm (offshore) Wave farm	L 4, L 5.2, L 6
Symbol	Wind motor visually conspicuous	L 5.1

Platforms and Moorings

Symbol	Offshore platform	L 10, L 17, L 2, L 12-15
Symbol	Conspicuous flare stack on offshore platform	L 11
Symbol	Installation buoy and mooring buoy, simplified	L 16

(installation buoy symbol)	Installation buoy, paper chart	L 16
(ground tackle symbol)	Ground tackle	L 18
Underwater Installations		
(5 in gray circle)	Underwater hazard with depth of 20 meters or less	L 20, L 21.2
(25 in dotted circle)	Underwater hazard with depth greater than 20 meters	L 20, L 21.2
(isolated danger symbol)	Isolated danger of depth less than the safety contour	L 20, L21.1-3
#	Foul area of seabed safe for navigation but not for anchoring	L 22
(square symbol)	Obstruction in the water which is always above water level	L 23
(turbine symbol with i box)	Underwater turbine or subsurface ODAS	L 24
(turbine symbol with i box)	Underwater turbine or subsurface ODAS	L 25
Submarine Cables		
(submarine cable line)	Submarine cable, status of disused is obtained by cursor pick	L 30.1, L 30.2, L 32
(submarine cable area box)	Submarine cable area	L 31.1, L 31.2
Submarine Pipelines		
(pipeline symbol)	Oil, gas pipeline, submerged or on land	L 40.1
(pipeline area box with i)	Submarine pipeline area with potentially dangerous contents	L 40.2
(pipeline symbol)	Water pipeline, sewer, etc.	L 41.1
(pipeline area box with i)	Submarine pipeline area with generally non-dangerous contents	L 41.2
(pipeline tunnel symbol)	Pipeline tunnel	L 42.2

—o —o ⦂3₂⦂	Underwater hazard with depth of 20 meters or less	L 43
—o —o ✕	Isolated danger of depth less than the safety contour	L 43

M. Tracks, Routes

Tracks

Leading line bearing a non-regulated, recommended track		
-<?>— — —<	Direction not encoded	M 1
— —<——270 deg<	One-way	M 1
—270 deg——<——>	Two-way	M 1
_ _ _270 deg_ _ _	Clearing line; transit line	M 2
Non-regulated, recommended track based on fixed marks		
-<?>— — —<	Direction not encoded	M 3, M 32.2
—>——90 deg——>	One-way	M 3, M 32.2
<—>—270 deg—<—>	Two-way	M 3, M 32.2
Non-regulated, recommended track not based on fixed marks		
-<?>— — —<	Direction not encoded	M 4
—>—90 deg— — >	One-way	M 4
-<—>—270 deg— —<-	Two-way	M 4
Based on fixed marks, one-way		
—>——90 deg——>	Non-regulated recommended track	M 5.1
—>— DW —>	Deep water route	M 5.1
Not based on fixed marks, one-way		
—>—90 deg— — >	Non-regulated recommended track	M 5.2
—>— DW —	Deep water route centerline	M 5.2

Routing Measures *[See Section 2.11.]*

➡	Traffic direction in a one-way lane of a traffic separation scheme	M 10
⊏- - ⊳	Single traffic direction in a two-way route part of a traffic separation scheme	M 11
▬▬▬▬	Traffic separation line	M 12

	Traffic separation zone	M 13
	Traffic separation scheme boundary	M 15
	Traffic precautionary area as a point	M 16
	Traffic precautionary area as an area *[Cross-hatching and border symbols only appear when stylized display is chosen.]*	M 16
	Axis and boundary of archipelagic sea lane	M 17
	Fairway, depth is obtained by cursor pick	M 18

Radar Surveillance Systems

	Radar station	M 30
	Radar range	M 31
270 deg	Radar line	M 32.1

Radio Reporting Points

Nr 13 ch s74	Radio calling-in point for traffic in one direction only	M 40.1
Nr 13 ch s74	Radio calling-in point for traffic in both directions	M 40.1
? Nr 13 ch s74	Radio calling-in point, direction not encoded	M 40.1
Nr 13 ch s74	Radio calling-in point for traffic in one direction only	M 40.2
Nr 13 ch s74	Radio calling-in point for traffic in both directions	M 40.2
Nr 13 ch s74	Radio calling-in point, direction not encoded	M 40.2

Ferries *[See Section 2.11.]*		
– ⬭ – – – ⊏	Ferry route	M 50
– ⬭ – – – ⊏	Cable ferry route	M 51

Examples of Routing Measures *[Displayed on following diagram.]*	
(18)	Safety fairway
(20.1)	Traffic Separation Scheme (TSS), traffic separated by separation zone
(20.2)	Traffic Separation Scheme, traffic separated by natural obstructions
(20.3)	Traffic Separation Scheme, with outer separation zone separating traffic using scheme from traffic not using it
(21)	Traffic Separation Scheme, roundabout with separation zone
(22)	Traffic Separation Scheme, with "crossing gates"
(23)	Traffic Separation Scheme crossing, without designated precautionary area
(24)	Precautionary area
(25.1)	Inshore Traffic Zone (ITZ), with defined end limits
(25.2)	Inshore Traffic Zone, without defined end limits
(26.1)	Recommended direction of traffic flow, between traffic separation schemes
(26.2)	Recommended direction of traffic flow,
(27.1)	Deep Water Route (DW), as part of a one-way traffic lane
(27.2)	Two-way deep water route, with minimum depth stated
(27.3)	Deep water route, centerline as recommended one-way or two-way track
(28.1)	Recommended route, one-way and two-way (often marked by centerline buoys)
(28.2)	Two-way route, with one-way sections
(29.1)	Area to be Avoided (ATBA), around navigational aid
(29.2)	Area to be Avoided, e.g. because of danger of stranding

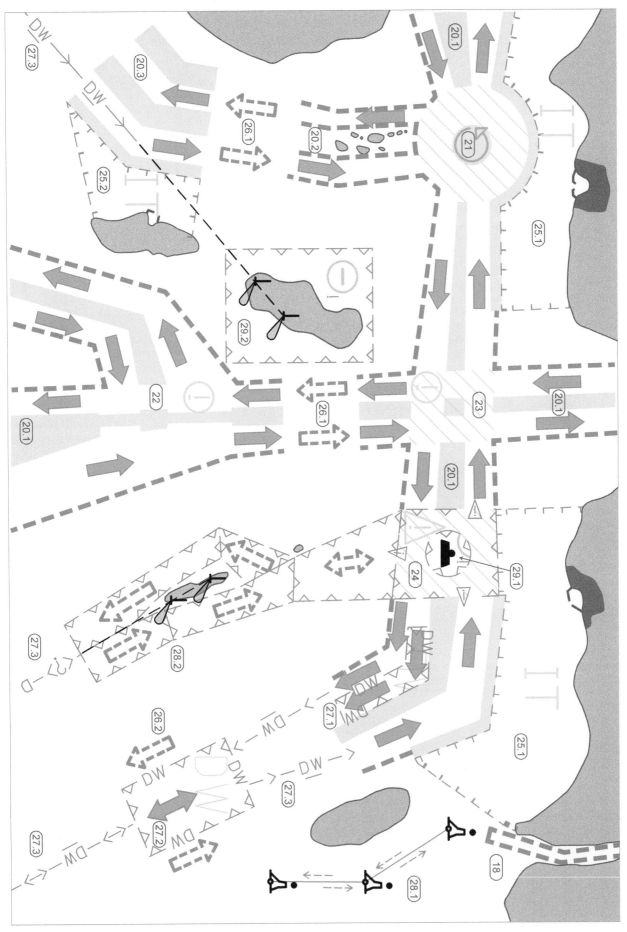

N. Areas, Limits

[Access to chart notes that are often crucial to these objects is discussed in Section 2.12. Land areas and regions are considered Natural and Cultural Features.]

General		
ECDIS represents many types of area limits with just a few different symbols. Information about the type of area and its associated restrictions or prohibitions may be obtained by cursor pick.		
	Caution area, a specific caution note applies	N 1.1, N 1.2
	Area where entry is prohibited or restricted or to be avoided *[An "i", if present means additional information is available; an "!" means other cautions apply.]*	N 2.1, N 2.2
Anchorages, Anchorage Areas		
	Anchorage area as a point at small scale, or anchor points of mooring trot at large scale	N 10
Nr 6	Anchor berth	N 11.1
	Type of anchorage area is obtained by cursor pick	N 12.1-9
Note: Anchors as part of the limit symbol are not shown for small areas. Other types of anchorage areas may be shown.		
	Seaplane landing area	N 13
Restricted Areas *Section 2.11*		
	Area where anchoring is prohibited or restricted *[An "i", if present means additional information is available; an "!" means other cautions apply.]*	N 20

	Area where fishing or trawling is prohibited or restricted *[An "i", if present means additional information is available; an "!" means other cautions apply.]*	N 21.1
	Area where diving is prohibited	N 21.2
	Environmentally Sensitive Sea Area (ESSA)	N 22.1-3
	Area with minor restrictions or information notices	N 22.1-3
	Particularly Sensitive Sea Area (PSSA)	N 22.4
	Explosives or chemical dumping ground as a point	N 23.1
	Explosives or chemical dumping ground as an area	N 23.2, N 24
	Degaussing area	N 25
Military Practice Areas		
	Restricted area	N 30, N 32, N 33
	Area where entry is prohibited or restricted or to be avoided, with other cautions. Minefield	N 31, N 34
International Boundaries and National Limits		
	Jurisdiction boundary	N 40, N 41
	Straight territorial sea baseline Custom regulation zone	N 42, N 48

– – – – – – –	Territorial sea Contiguous zone Limits of fishery zone Continental shelf area Exclusive economic zone	N 43-47
▽ ▽ ▽	Harbor area, symbolized	N 49

Various Limits

	Continuous pattern for an ice area (glacier, etc.)	N 60.1, N 60.2
⊗	Floating hazard	N 61
– – – – – –	Boom, ice boom	N 61
(⊗)	Boom, ice boom, floating obstruction, log pond	N 61
i	HO information note	N 62.1, N 62.2, N 64, N 65
!	Dredging area	N 63

P. Lights

[Typical attributes of lights include: category, color, characteristic, group, period, sectors, nominal range, height, name, exhibition condition, multiplicity, name, system of navigational marks, among others. Lights can be located on buoys, beacons, landmarks, or single buildings.]

Light Structures and Major Floating Lights *[See Section 2.9.]*

	Light, lighthouse, paper chart	P 1
	Light, lighthouse, paper chart	P 1
	Lighted offshore platform, paper chart	P 2
	Lighted beacon tower, paper chart	P 3

	Lighted beacon, paper chart	P 4, P 5
	Light vessel, paper chart	P 6

Light Characters *[See Section 2.9.]*

When text for lights is displayed, ECDIS uses INT abbreviations.		P 10.1-11, P 12-14
	Default light symbol if no color is encoded or color is other than red, green, white, yellow, amber, or orange	P 11.1-8
	Red	P 11.1-8
	Green	P 11.1-8
	White, yellow, amber or orange	P 11.1-8
	Sector Lights	P 11.1-8

Example of a Full Light Description

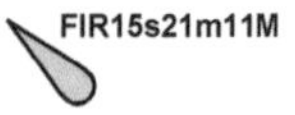 FlR15s21m11M	The descriptions of non-sector lights are shown in ECDIS when the display of text is turned on, as shown. (The aid to navigation or other structure that is always shown attached to a light flare in ECDIS is not depicted here.)	P 16
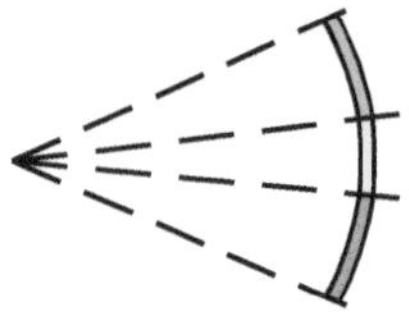	Sector lights (as described in the INT, NOAA and NGA examples at left) are depicted graphically in ECDIS, as shown here and in P40.	P 16

Lights Marking Fairways

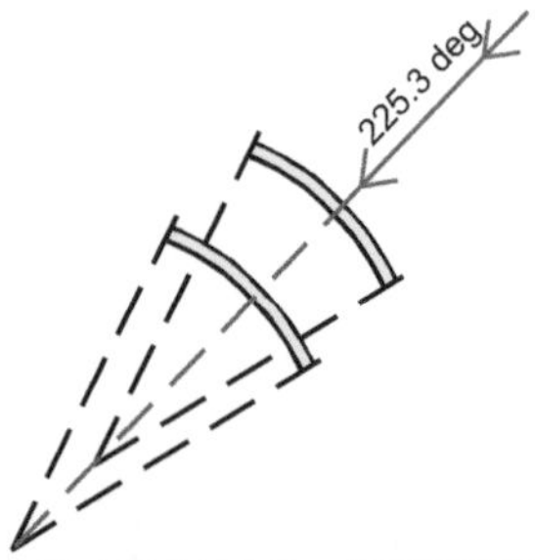	Leading lights with sectors	P 20.1
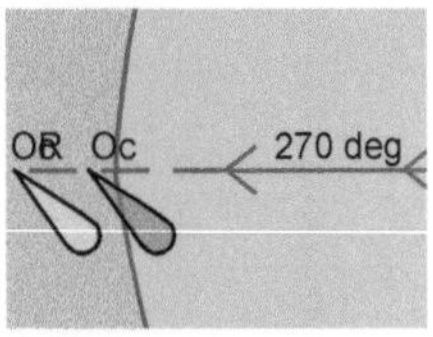	Leading lights	P 20.2

	Lights in line, marking the sides of a channel	P 21

Direction Lights

	Directional light with sector	P30.1
	Directional light without sector	P 30.2
	Light, directional	P 30.3, P 30.4
	Category of light as moiré effect is obtained by cursor pick	P 31

Sector Lights *[See Section 2.9.]*

	Light, sector	P 40.1, P 40.2
	Light, danger	P 42

	Light, obscured	P 43
	Light, restricted	P 44
	Light, faint	P 45
	Light, intensified	P 46
Special Lights		
AeroAlFlWG7.5s11M	Light	P 60
AeroFR313m11M	Conspicuous mast with light	P 61.1, P 61.2
◯⟨	Floodlight	P 63
/\/\	Strip light	P 64

ECDIS Traditional (Paper Chart) and ECDIS Simplified Symbols

ECDIS can be set to display aids to navigation with either traditional paper chart symbols or what they call "simplified symbols." The two symbol sets are shown here. Some ECDIS color fill the paper chart buoy shapes, but this is not required by IHO ECDIS specifications.

[Simplified cardinal buoy symbols have an IHO specified outline thickness that is twice that of cardinal beacons, but individual ECS or ECDIS displays may not reflect this.]

[On both paper charts and ECDIS displays, floating objects are tilted, whereas fixed beacons are shown vertical—a convention that helps us interpret the symbols. Even the labels are tilted (italics) to support the convention.]

Floating Marks *[See Section 2.7.]*		
Paper Chart	Simplified	Simplified Symbol name
		Cardinal buoy, north
		Cardinal buoy, east
		Cardinal buoy, south
		Cardinal buoy, west
		Default symbol for buoy (used when no defining attributes have been encoded in the ENC)
		Isolated danger buoy
		Conical lateral buoy, green
		Conical lateral buoy, red
		Can shape lateral buoy, green
		Can shape lateral buoy, red
		Installation buoy and mooring buoy
**		Safe water buoy
		Special purpose buoy, spherical or barrel shaped, or default symbol for special purpose buoy
		Special purpose TSS buoy marking the starboard side of the traffic lane
		Special purpose TSS buoy marking the port side of the traffic lane
		Special purpose ice buoy or spar or pillar shaped buoy
		Super-buoy ODAS & LANBY
		Light float
		Light vessel

Fixed Marks *[See Section 1.7, 2.9.]*

Paper Chart	Simplified	Simplified Symbol name
		Cardinal beacon, north
		Cardinal beacon, east
		Cardinal beacon, south
		Cardinal beacon, west
?	?	Default symbol for beacon (used when no defining attributes have been encoded in the ENC)
		Isolated danger beacon
		Major lateral beacon, red
		Major lateral beacon, green
		Minor lateral beacon, green
		Major safe water beacon *[Major beacon symbols are used for tower, lattice, and pile beacons, specified in the attribute beacon shape (BCNSHP).]*
		Minor safe water beacon
		Major special purpose beacon
		Minor special purpose beacon

* Paper chart symbols display various buoy or beacon shape symbols in conjunction with the topmark.

** Several different paper chart symbols correspond to this simplified symbol

Day Marks

Paper Chart	Simplified	Simplified Symbol name
		Square or rectangular daymark
		Triangular daymark, point up
		Triangular daymark, point down
		Retro Reflector

Q. Buoys, Beacons

[Typical Attributes of Buoys and Beacons: Shape, Color, Color Pattern, Condition, Radar Conspicuous, Visually Conspicuous, Height, System of Navigational Marks, Nature of Construction, Object Name, among others.]

Buoys and Beacons

Ω?	Default symbol for buoy, paper chart	
⊙?	Default symbol for buoy, simplified	
↓?	Default symbol for a beacon, paper chart	
▯?	Default symbol for a beacon, simplified	
ECDIS shows the position of buoys and beacons with a circle at the bottom of paper chart symbols. For simplified symbols, the position of the aid corresponds with the center of the symbol.		Q 1

Colors of Buoys and Beacon Topmarks

⊨	Retro reflector	Q 6

Topmarks and Radar Reflectors*

Paper chart symbols for topmarks are always displayed above a buoy or beacon shape symbol, as in Q 10 and Q 11. Simplified symbols for cardinal marks, isolated dangers, and safe water, consist of only the topmark without the buoy shape symbol. Simplified symbology for marks with any other type of topmark will display on the simplified buoy or beacon shape symbol without a topmark.

Paper Chart	Simplified		
▲▲	◿◿	2 cones point upward	Q 9
▲▼	◿▽	2 cones point downward	Q 9
▼▼	▽▽	2 cones base to base	Q 9
▼▲	▽◿	2 cones point to point	Q 9
●●	○○	2 spheres	Q 9
●	⊙	Sphere	Q 9
▲		Cone point up	Q 9
▼		Cone point down	Q 9
▯		Cylinder, square, vertical rectangle	Q 9
✕		X-shape	Q 9
/		Flag or other shape	Q 9
▭		Board, horizontal rectangle	Q 9
◆		Cube point up	Q 9

┼		Upright cross over a circle	Q 9
⊤		T-shape	Q 9
bn No 2		Beacon in general with topmark, paper chart	Q 10
by No 3		Conical buoy with topmark, paper chart	Q 11

*ECDIS does not display radar reflectors on fixed or floating aids; this information is obtained by cursor pick.

Shapes of Buoys *[See Section 2.7.]*

Paper Chart	Simplified		
		Conical buoy	Q 20
		Can buoy	Q 21
		Spherical buoy	Q 22
		Pillar Buoy	Q 23
		Spar Buoy	Q 24
		Barrel Buoy	Q 25
		Super-buoy	Q 26
		Lanby, super-buoy	Q 26
		Super-buoy odas & lanby	Q 26

Minor Light Floats *[See Section 2.9.]*

Paper Chart	Simplified		
		Light float	Q 30
		Light float	Q 31

Mooring Buoys *[See Section 2.7.]*

	Mooring buoy, can shape, paper chart	Q 40
	Mooring buoy, barrel shape, paper chart	Q 40
	Installation buoy and mooring buoy, simplified	Q 40
	Mooring buoy with light flare, barrel shape, paper chart	Q 41

	Trot, mooring buoys with ground tackle and berth numbers	Q 42
	Mooring buoy, can shape, paper chart *[with telegraphic or telephonic communication]*	Q 43
	Mooring buoy, barrel shape, paper chart *[with telegraphic or telephonic communication]*	Q 43
	Installation buoy and mooring buoy, simplified *[with telegraphic or telephonic communication]*	Q 43
	Small craft mooring area	Q 44
	Availability of visitor moorings at marina is obtained by cursor pick	Q 45

Special Purpose Buoys *[See Section 2.7.]*

	Conical buoy with topmark, paper chart	Q 50-57, Q 59, Q 62
	Special purpose buoy, spherical or barrel shaped, or default symbol for special purpose buoy, simplified	Q 50-59
	Super-buoy, paper chart	Q 58
	Super-buoy odas & lanby simplified	Q 58
	Spherical buoy, paper chart	Q 58
	Conical buoy, paper chart	Q 60

Beacons *[See Section 1.7, 2.9.]*

	Default symbol for a beacon, paper chart	Q 80
	Default symbol for a beacon, simplified	Q 80
	Beacon in general, paper chart	Q 80
	Beacon in general with topmark, paper chart	Q 82
	Major red lateral beacon, simplified	Q 82
	Beacon in general with topmark, paper chart	Q 82

△ (over) △	Cardinal beacon, north, simplified	Q 82
● ● ⬥	Beacon in general with topmark, paper chart	Q 82, Q 83
○ ○	Isolated danger beacon, simplified	Q 82, Q 83
Minor Impermanent Marks Usually in Drying Areas (Lateral Marks of Minor Channels)		
⊥	Minor, stake or pole beacon, paper chart	Q 90-92
▯	Minor red lateral beacon, simplified	Q 91, Q 92
▯	Minor green lateral beacon, simplified	Q 91, Q 92
Minor Marks, Usually on Land		
⧉	Conspicuous cairn	Q 100
⊡	Square or rectangular day mark, paper chart	Q 101
⊡	Square or rectangular day mark, simplified	Q 101
△	Triangular day mark, point up, paper chart	Q 101
△	Triangular day mark, point up, simplified	Q 101
▽	Triangular day mark, point down, paper chart	Q 101
▽	Triangular day mark, point down, simplified	Q 101
Beacon Towers *Section 1.7, 2.9*		
⌂	Beacon tower, paper chart	Q 110
◻⌂ ▲⌂ / ▲⌂ ●⌂	Beacon tower with topmarks, paper chart	Q 110
▮	Major red lateral beacon, simplified	Q 110
▯	Major green lateral beacon, simplified	Q 110
⬚	Lattice beacon, paper chart	Q 111
Special Purpose Beacons		
↓ — ↓ 270 deg ←	Leading beacons	Q 120
↓ — ↓ 270 deg —	Beacons marking a clearing line or transit	Q 121

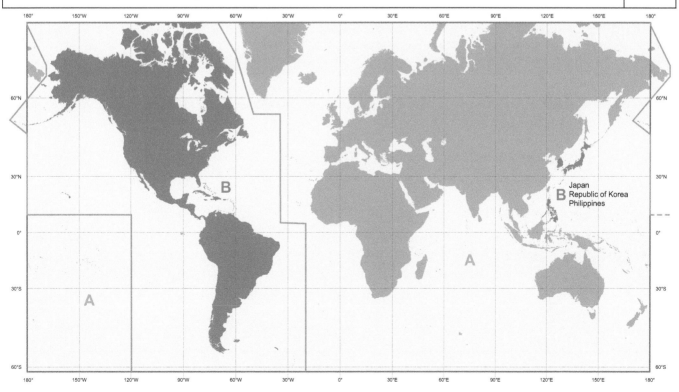	Beacons marking measured distance	Q 122
	Cable landing beacon (example)	Q 123
	Notice board	Q 126

IALA Maritime Buoyage System	
IALA International Association of Marine Aids to Navigation and Lighthouse Authorities	
Where in force, the IALA System applies to all fixed and floating marks except landfall lights, leading lights and marks, sectored lights and major floating lights. The standard buoy shapes are cylindrical (can) ⌐, conical ⌂, spherical ⌂, pillar ⌘, and spar ∤, but variations may occur, for example: light floats ⌐. In the illustrations in Q 130.1, only the standard buoy shapes are used. In the case of fixed beacons (lit or unlit), only the shape of the topmark is of navigational significance. Lateral marks are generally for well-defined channels.	Q 130
There are two international buoyage regions where lateral marks differ. Region A is primarily comprised of the waters surrounding Greenland, Africa, Europe, Australia and Asia (except for Japan, the Republic of Korea and the Philippines). Region B is primarily comprised of the waters surrounding North and South America, Japan, the Republic of Korea and the Philippines.	
ECDIS marks the boundary between IALA regions A and B with this symbol:	
— A — — B — — A — — B — — A — — B — — A — — B — — A — — B —	
[The attribute system of navigational marks is given for many objects on the chart.]	

Direction of Buoyage

The direction of buoyage is that taken when approaching a harbor from seaward. Along coasts, the direction is determined by buoyage authorities, normally clockwise around land masses.

Symbols showing direction of buoyage where it is not obvious

	General symbol for direction of buoyage	Q 130.2
	IALA Region A	Q 130.2
	IALA Region B	Q 130.2

Cardinal Marks [See Section 2.7.]

Indicating navigable water to the named side of the marks. In the illustration below all marks are the same in Regions A and B.

	Paper chart symbology	Q 130.3
	Simplified symbology	Q 130.3

Isolated Danger Marks		
Stationed over dangers with navigable water around them.		
	Pillar buoy with 2 spheres topmark	Q 130.4
	Spar buoy with 2 spheres topmark	Q 130.4
	Isolated danger buoy, simplified	Q 130.4
Safe Water Marks		
Such as mid-channel and landfall marks.		
	Spherical buoy, paper chart	Q 130.5
	Pillar buoy with sphere topmark	Q 130.5
	Spar buoy with sphere topmark	Q 130.5
	Safe water buoy, simplified	Q 130.5
Special Marks		
Not primarily to assist navigation but to indicate special features.		
	Spherical buoy, paper chart	Q 130.5
	Can buoy	Q 130.6
	Conical buoy	Q 130.6
	Spar buoy with x-shape topmark	Q 130.6
	Special purpose buoy, simplified	Q 130.6

R. Fog Signals

General [*See Section 2.7.*]		
⊙	Position of a conspicuous point feature with fog signal	R 1
	Lighted pillar buoy, paper chart with fog signal	R 1
	Lighted super-buoy, paper chart with fog signal	R 1
Examples of Fog Signal Descriptions		
Note: The fog signal symbol will usually be omitted when a description of the signal is given.		
	Light with fog signal	R 20
	Pillar buoy, paper chart with fog signal	R 21

Paper Chart	Simplified		
		Lighted pillar buoy, with fog signal	R 22

S. Radar, Radio, Satellite Navigation Systems

Radar		
◯	**Radar station** [*The S-52 explanation of this symbol is "Radio Station" but it is used to depict both radio stations and radar stations. Use cursor pick.*]	S 1
◌	Radar transponder beacon	S 2, S 3.1-5

Paper Chart	Simplified		
		Radar transponder on floating mark	S 3.6
	☼	Symbol indicating this object is radar conspicuous	S 4, S 5

Radio

	Radio station	S 10-16

Additional information regarding radio, such as category of radio station, signal frequency, communication channel, call sign, estimated signal range, periodicity and status may be included in the cursor pick.

The presence of an AIS transmitted signal intended for use as an aid to navigation associated with a physical aid, including the AIS MMSI Number, can be obtained by cursor pick on the physical aid.

	North cardinal virtual aid	S 18.2

Satellite Navigation Systems

	DGPS reference station	S 51

T. Services

Pilotage

	Pilot boarding place	T 1.1-4
	Pilot boarding area	T 1.1-4

Coast Guard, Rescue

	Coast Guard station	T 10, T 11
	Rescue station	T 11-14

Signal Stations

	Signal station	T 20-36

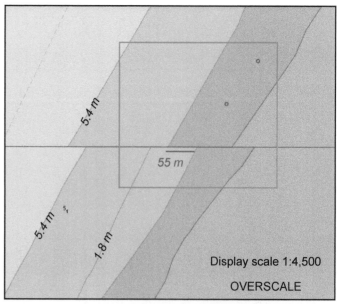

Appendix

Appendix 1. Chart Accuracy and Overscaling

Chart accuracy is discussed in Section 2.4 and overscale (also called over-zoomed) is discussed in Section 2.3. This section illustrates these points. This is not a exact cartographic analysis, but just a way to get a feeling for the issue at hand, namely, overscaling can present a chart that appears more accurate than it is. We start by looking at a case where we know something is wrong.

Figure A1-1 shows the two adjacent ENC cells that are the only charts of the coastline shown. There is no ZOC accuracy data in either one, but referring to the RNC counterparts we learn from the source diagrams that the surveys of the narrow strip along the coast are category B3, dated 1940 to 1969. These data have larger uncertainties than modern surveys, and the discrepancies we see in Figure A1-2 are consistent with this. The mismatch could be even larger on other charts.

The point here is, over-zooming on these chart boundaries can illustrate this discrepancy in accuracy, whereas in other places it would not at all be obvious. Figure A1-3 and A1-4 show examples where we would want to take care in heeding the stated charting uncertainties.

Remember, however, that just because chart data has a stated uncertainty of some amount does not mean it is wrong by that amount. Indeed, position measurements in surveys of this "B3 period" were made by horizontal sextant piloting, which can be more accurate than what we might dependably assign to standard GPS (± 20 m). In fact, we will be amazed much more often by NOAA chart accuracy than by a lack of accuracy.

[GPS can be and often is remarkably better than noted above; this "standard" value accounts for situations with no differential corrections (DGPS) and considers the often unaccounted for location of the GPS antenna on the vessel, not to mention that high nearby terrain can limit signal quality. For a practical look at this, when tied up at the dock, turn on your GPS, set the tracking to plot your position every 30 seconds, and let it run overnight. Then zoom in on the results in the morning to see where all you have been and where you were most of the time.]

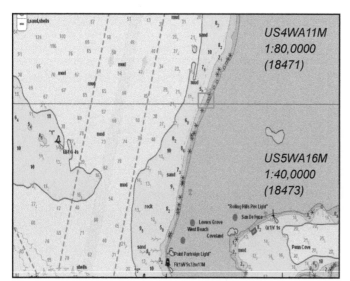

Figure A1-1. *Two adjacent ENC cells. The red box marks the area shown in Figure A1-2.*

Figure A1-2. *A much overscaled view showing discontinuity at the boundary. The 55 m shown is consistent with the B3 survey shown on both of the RNCs. The top ENC does not include a 1.8 m contour, so that one just ends at the boundary..*

Figure A1-3 is from an ENC with no accuracy included, but the corresponding paper charts show it is the same B3 level discussed earlier. There is really nothing special about this example. Almost any chart could be over-zoomed like this, to the point where the chart still looks perfectly good, but the uncertainties in the locations of the objects shown are larger than those of the vessel itself.

Figure A1-4 is a U.S. ENC of an area in Panama, which can be seen in the MACHC viewer online. This chart could be as accurate as implied in the this much overscaled view, but this ENC includes a zone of confidence (ZOC) category of "D," which is defined as position uncertainty "Worse than C," which in turn is ± 478 m. In a case like this, it would be valuable to check the chart in several places before relying on it to much extent. Horizontal sextant angles are one way to check the GPS, or crossed azimuth lines obtained in some manner. Appendix A5 shows the best way to obtain the most likely position from three lines of position, taking into account the uncertainty in each of those.

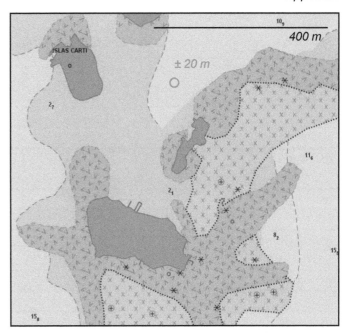

Figure A1-4. *An overscaled view (x7.7) of US509890 (an NGA chart converted to ENC) with a ZOC value of "D." We might interpret that as intending to convey a stronger message than having object quality of data (M_QUAL) simply listed as "U (data not assessed)."*

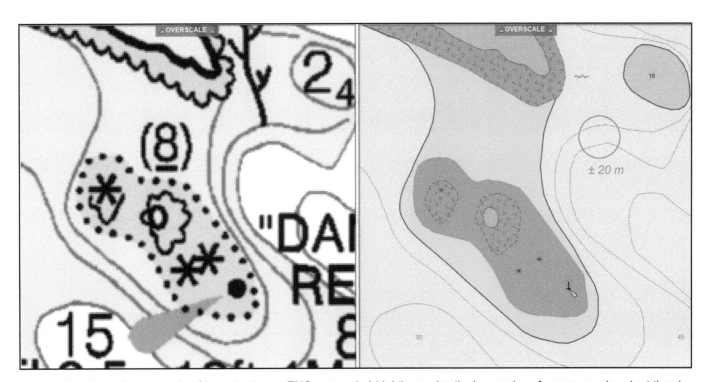

Figure A1-3. *A random example of how viewing an ENC overscaled (right) can give the impression of a more precise chart than is justified by its documented survey period. At the same time, we might not be so tempted when viewing the best RNC of the area shown on the left. This chart is also B3 survey era, with stated uncertainties that are larger than the ± 20 m shown to represent a typical, or at least possible, GPS uncertainty.*

Appendix 2. ENC Country Codes

Listed below are the nations that produce ENCs and the codes used to identify their products in the chart names. Each of these producers has a web page that is listed in the member section of the IHO.

Name	Code	Name	Code	Name	Code
Argentina	AR	Kuwait	KW	UK	GB
Australia	AU	Latvia	LV	Ukraine	UA
Bahrain	BH	Malaysia	MY	United Arab Emirates	AE
Bangladesh	BD	Mauritius	MU	Uruguay	UY
Belgium	BE	Mexico	MX	USA	US
Brazil	BR	Monaco	MC	Venezuela	VE
Brunei Darussalam	BN	Montenegro	ME	Viet Nam	VN
Cameroon	CM	Morocco	MA		
Canada	CA	Mozambique	MZ		
Chile	CL	Myanmar	MM		
China	CN	Netherlands	NL		
Colombia	CO	New Zealand	NZ		
Congo (Dem. Rep. of)	CD	Nigeria	NG		
Croatia	HR	Norway	NO		
Cuba	CU	Oman	OM		
Cyprus	CY	Pakistan	PK		
Denmark	DK	Papua New Guinea	PG		
Dominican Rep.	DO	Peru	PE		
Ecuador	EC	Philippines	PH		
Egypt	EG	Poland	PL		
Estonia	EE	Portugal	PT		
Fiji	FJ	Qatar	QA		
Finland	FI	Romania	RO		
France	FR	Russian Federation	RU		
Georgia	GE	Saudi Arabia	SA		
Germany	DE	Serbia	RS		
Greece	GR	Singapore	SG		
Guatemala	GT	Slovenia	SI		
Iceland	IS	South Africa (Rep. of)	ZA		
India	IN	Spain	ES		
India	I7	Sri Lanka	LK		
Indonesia	ID	Suriname	SR		
Ireland	IE	Sweden	SE		
Islamic Rep. of Iran	IR	Syrian Arab Republic	SY		
Italy	IT	Thailand	TH		
Jamaica	JM	Tonga	TO		
Japan	JP	Trinidad & Tobago	TT		
Korea (DPR of)	KP	Tunisia	TN		
Korea (Rep. of)	KR	Turkey	TR		

Appendix 3. S-57 OBJECTS

OBJECT	ACRONYM
Administration Area (Named)	ADMARE
Airport/airfield	AIRARE
Anchor berth	ACHBRT
Anchorage area	ACHARE
Beacon, cardinal	BCNCAR
Beacon, isolated danger	BCNISD
Beacon, lateral	BCNLAT
Beacon, safe water	BCNSAW
Beacon, special purpose/general	BCNSPP
Berth	BERTHS
Bridge	BRIDGE
Building, single	BUISGL
Built-up area	BUAARE
Buoy, cardinal	BOYCAR
Buoy, installation	BOYINB
Buoy, isolated danger	BOYISD
Buoy, lateral	BOYLAT
Buoy, safe water	BOYSAW
Buoy, special purpose/general	BOYSPP
Cable area	CBLARE
Cable, overhead	CBLOHD
Cable, submarine	CBLSUB
Canal	CANALS
Canal bank	CANBNK
Cargo transhipment area	CTSARE
Causeway	CAUSWY
Caution area	CTNARE
Checkpoint	CHKPNT
Coastguard station	CGUSTA
Coastline	COALNE
Contiguous zone	CONZNE
Continental shelf area	COSARE
Control point	CTRPNT
Conveyor	CONVYR
Crane	CRANES
Current - non-gravitational	CURENT
Custom zone	CUSZNE
Dam	DAMCON
Daymark	DAYMAR
Deep water route centerline	DWRTCL
Deep water route part	DWRTPT
Depth area	DEPARE
Depth contour	DEPCNT
Distance mark	DISMAR
Dock area	DOCARE

OBJECT	ACRONYM
Dredged area	DRGARE
Dry dock	DRYDOC
Dumping ground	DMPGRD
Dyke	DYKCON
Exclusive economic zone	EXEZNE
Fairway	FAIRWY
Fence/wall	FNCLNE
Ferry route	FERYRT
Fishery zone	FSHZNE
Fishing facility	FSHFAC
Fishing ground	FSHGRD
Floating dock	FLODOC
Fog signal	FOGSIG
Fortified structure	FORSTC
Free port area	FRPARE
Gate	GATCON
Gridiron	GRIDRN
Harbour area (administrative)	HRBARE
Harbour facility	HRBFAC
Hulk	HULKES
Ice area	ICEARE
Incineration area	ICNARE
Inshore traffic zone	ISTZNE
Lake	LAKARE
Lake shore	LAKSHR
Land area	LNDARE
Land elevation	LNDELV
Land region	LNDRGN
Landmark	LNDMRK
Light	LIGHTS
Light float	LITFLT
Light vessel	LITVES
Local magnetic anomaly	LOCMAG
Lock basin	LOKBSN
Log pond	LOGPON
Magnetic variation	MAGVAR
Marine farm/culture	MARCUL
Military practice area	MIPARE
Mooring/Warping facility	MORFAC
Navigation line	NAVLNE
Obstruction	OBSTRN
Offshore platform	OFSPLF
Offshore production area	OSPARE
Oil barrier	OILBAR
Pile	PILPNT

OBJECT	ACRONYM	OBJECT	ACRONYM
Pilot boarding place	PILBOP	Tidal stream - harmonic prediction	TS_PRH
Pipeline area	PIPARE	Tidal stream - non-harmonic prediction	TS_PNH
Pipeline, overhead	PIPOHD	Tidal stream panel data	TS_PAD
Pipeline, submarine/on land	PIPSOL	Tidal stream - time series	TS_TIS
Pontoon	PONTON	Tide - harmonic prediction	T_HMON
Precautionary area	PRCARE	Tide - non-harmonic prediction	T_NHMN
Production/storage area	PRDARE	Tide - time series	T_TIMS
Pylon/bridge support	PYLONS	Tideway	TIDEWY
Radar line	RADLNE	Topmark	TOPMAR
Radar range	RADRNG	Traffic separation line	TSELNE
Radar reflector	RADRFL	Traffic separation scheme boundary	TSSBND
Radar station	RADSTA	Traffic separation scheme crossing	TSSCRS
Radar transponder beacon	RTPBCN	Traffic separation scheme lane part	TSSLPT
Radio calling-in point	RDOCAL	Traffic separation scheme roundabout	TSSRON
Radio station	RDOSTA	Traffic separation zone	TSEZNE
Railway	RAILWY	Tunnel	TUNNEL
Rapids	RAPIDS	Two-way route part	TWRTPT
Recommended route centerline	RCRTCL	Underwater/awash rock	UWTROC
Recommended track	RECTRC	Unsurveyed area	UNSARE
Recommended traffic lane part	RCTLPT	Vegetation	VEGATN
Rescue station	RSCSTA	Water turbulence	WATTUR
Restricted area	RESARE	Waterfall	WATFAL
Retro-reflector	RETRFL	Weed/Kelp	WEDKLP
River	RIVERS	Wreck	WRECKS
River bank	RIVBNK	Accuracy of data	M_ACCY
Road	ROADWY	Compilation scale of data	M_CSCL
Runway	RUNWAY	Coverage	M_COVR
Sand waves	SNDWAV	Horizontal datum of data	M_HDAT
Sea area/named water area	SEAARE	Horizontal datum shift parameters	M_HOPA
Sea-plane landing area	SPLARE	Nautical publication information	M_NPUB
Seabed area	SBDARE	Navigational system of marks	M_NSYS
Shoreline construction	SLCONS	Production information	M_PROD
Signal station, traffic	SISTAT	Quality of data	M_QUAL
Signal station, warning	SISTAW	Sounding datum	M_SDAT
Silo/tank	SILTNK	Survey reliability	M_SREL
Slope topline	SLOTOP	Units of measurement of data	M_UNIT
Sloping ground	SLOGRD	Vertical datum of data	M_VDAT
Small craft facility	SMCFAC	Aggregation	C_AGGR
Sounding	SOUNDG	Association	C_ASSO
Spring	SPRING	Stacked on/stacked under	C_STAC
Square	SQUARE	Cartographic area	$AREAS
Straight territorial sea baseline	STSLNE	Cartographic line	$LINES
Submarine transit lane	SUBTLN	Cartographic symbol	$CSYMB
Swept Area	SWPARE	Compass	$COMPS
Territorial sea area	TESARE	Text	$TEXTS
Tidal stream - flood/ebb	TS_FEB		

Appendix 4. S-57 ATTRIBUTES

ATTRIBUTE	ACRONYM
Agency responsible for production	AGENCY
Beacon shape	BCNSHP
Building shape	BUISHP
Buoy shape	BOYSHP
Buried depth	BURDEP
Call sign	CALSGN
Category of airport/airfield	CATAIR
Category of anchorage	CATACH
Category of bridge	CATBRG
Category of built-up area	CATBUA
Category of cable	CATCBL
Category of canal	CATCAN
Category of cardinal mark	CATCAM
Category of checkpoint	CATCHP
Category of coastline	CATCOA
Category of control point	CATCTR
Category of conveyor	CATCON
Category of coverage	CATCOV
Category of crane	CATCRN
Category of dam	CATDAM
Category of distance mark	CATDIS
Category of dock	CATDOC
Category of dumping ground	CATDPG
Category of fenceline	CATFNC
Category of ferry	CATFRY
Category of fishing facility	CATFIF
Category of fog signal	CATFOG
Category of fortified structure	CATFOR
Category of gate	CATGAT
Category of ice	CATICE
Category of installation buoy	CATINB
Category of land region	CATLND
Category of landmark	CATLMK
Category of lateral mark	CATLAM
Category of light	CATLIT
Category of marine farm/culture	CATMFA
Category of military practice area	CATMPA
Category of mooring/warping facility	CATMOR
Category of obstruction	CATOBS
Category of offshore platform	CATOFP
Category of oil barrier	CATOLB
Category of pile	CATPLE

ATTRIBUTE	ACRONYM
Category of pilot boarding place	CATPIL
Category of pipeline/pipe	CATPIP
Category of production area	CATPRA
Category of pylon	CATPYL
Category of quality of data	CATQUA
Category of radar station	CATRAS
Category of radar transponder beacon	CATRTB
Category of radio station	CATROS
Category of recommended track	CATTRK
Category of rescue station	CATRSC
Category of restricted area	CATREA
Category of road	CATROD
Category of runway	CATRUN
Category of sea area	CATSEA
Category of shoreline construction	CATSLC
Category of signal station, traffic	CATSIT
Category of signal station, warning	CATSIW
Category of silo/tank	CATSIL
Category of slope	CATSLO
Category of small craft facility	CATSCF
Category of special purpose mark	CATSPM
Category of Tidal Stream	CAT_TS
Category of Traffic Separation Scheme	CATTSS
Category of vegetation	CATVEG
Category of water turbulence	CATWAT
Category of weed/kelp	CATWED
Category of wreck	CATWRK
Category of zone of confidence in data	CATZOC
Character spacing	$SPACE
Character specification	$CHARS
Colour	COLOUR
Colour pattern	COLPAT
Communication channel	COMCHA
Compass size	$CSIZE
Compilation date	CPDATE
Compilation scale	CSCALE
Condition	CONDTN
Conspicuous, radar	CONRAD
Conspicuous, visually	CONVIS
Current velocity	CURVEL
Date end	DATEND
Date start	DATSTA

ATTRIBUTE	ACRONYM	ATTRIBUTE	ACRONYM
Depth range value 1	DRVAL1	Recording indication	RECIND
Depth range value 2	DRVAL2	Reference year for magnetic variation	RYRMGV
Depth units	DUNITS	Restriction	RESTRN
Elevation	ELEVAT	Scale maximum	SCAMAX
Estimated range of transmission	ESTRNG	Scale minimum	SCAMIN
Exhibition condition of light	EXCLIT	Scale value one	SCVAL1
Exposition of sounding	EXPSOU	Scale value two	SCVAL2
Function	FUNCTN	Sector limit one	SECTR1
Height	HEIGHT	Sector limit two	SECTR2
Height/length units	HUNITS	Shift parameters	SHIPAM
Horizontal accuracy	HORACC	Signal frequency	SIGFRQ
Horizontal clearance	HORCLR	Signal generation	SIGGEN
Horizontal length	HORLEN	Signal group	SIGGRP
Horizontal width	HORWID	Signal period	SIGPER
Ice factor	ICEFAC	Signal sequence	SIGSEQ
Information	INFORM	Sounding accuracy	SOUACC
Jurisdiction	JRSDTN	Sounding distance - maximum	SDISMX
Justification - horizontal	$JUSTH	Sounding distance - minimum	SDISMN
Justification - vertical	$JUSTV	Source date	SORDAT
Lifting capacity	LIFCAP	Source indication	SORIND
Light characteristic	LITCHR	Status	STATUS
Light visibility	LITVIS	Survey date - end	SUREND
Marks navigational - System of	MARSYS	Survey date - start	SURSTA
Multiplicity of lights	MLTYLT	Survey type	SURTYP
Nationality	NATION	Symbol scaling factor	$SCALE
Nature of construction	NATCON	Symbolization code	$SCODE
Nature of surface	NATSUR	Technique of sounding measurement	TECSOU
Nature of surface - qualifying terms	NATQUA	Text string	$TXSTR
Notice to Mariners date	NMDATE	Textual description	TXTDSC
Object name	OBJNAM	Tidal stream - panel values	TS_TSP
Orientation	ORIENT	Tidal stream - time series values	TS_TSV
Periodic date end	PEREND	Tide - accuracy of water level	T_ACWL
Periodic date start	PERSTA	Tide - high and low water values	T_HWLW
Pictorial representation	PICREP	Tide - method of tidal prediction	T_MTOD
Pilot district	PILDST	Tide - time and height differences	T_THDF
Positional accuracy units	PUNITS	Tide - time series values	T_TSVL
Producing country	PRCTRY	Tide - value of harmonic constituents	T_VAHC
Product	PRODCT	Tide - time interval of values	T_TINT
Publication reference	PUBREF	Time end	TIMEND
Quality of sounding measurement	QUASOU	Time start	TIMSTA
Radar wave length	RADWAL	Tint	$TINTS
Radius	RADIUS	Topmark/daymark shape	TOPSHP
Recording date	RECDAT	Traffic flow	TRAFIC

ATTRIBUTE	ACRONYM
Value of annual change in magnetic variation	VALACM
Value of depth contour	VALDCO
Value of local magnetic anomaly	VALLMA
Value of magnetic variation	VALMAG
Value of maximum range	VALMXR
Value of nominal range	VALNMR
Value of sounding	VALSOU
Vertical accuracy	VERACC
Vertical clearance	VERCLR
Vertical clearance, closed	VERCCL
Vertical clearance, open	VERCOP

ATTRIBUTE	ACRONYM
Vertical clearance, safe	VERCSA
Vertical datum	VERDAT
Vertical length	VERLEN
Water level effect	WATLEV
Information in national language	NINFOM
Object name in national language	NOBJNM
Pilot district in national language	NPLDST
Text string in national language	$NTXST
Textual description in national language	NTXTDS
Horizontal datum	HORDAT
Positional Accuracy	POSACC
Quality of position	QUAPOS

Appendix 5. Most Likely Position from 3 LOPs*

In several places in the book, the issue of checking the GPS position (or having to rely on other sources) has come up, as it would in any prudent discussion of navigation. Often we can get by with basic accuracy for these checks, but occasionally we want to do the very best we can. The fixes we can do on our own, however, are always some form of piloting, which means we are finding our position relative to other locations that we have to assume are correct.

Short of celestial navigation, which is limited to about ± 0.5 nmi in good conditions and therefore not often adequate for inland navigation, we cannot find our latitude and longitude independent of the chart we are working on. With trusted landmarks in sight, however, we can do very precise fixes relative to them by several means, competing or exceeding standard GPS accuracy. All high accuracy piloting boils down to interpreting the lines (or circles) of position we measured. Once we have more than two (which is required) they will not intersect in a single point, but rather they will form a triad of three intersections and our task is to interpret that triangle of intersections for the best fix. This is a standard navigation problem that has existed since the inception of charting.

The following solution is readily solved on paper or directly on the ECS screen using electronic plotting tools.

• • •

Practicing navigators tend to choose the best position within a triad of intersecting LOPs (cocked hat) as a centroid value of their choice, based on their experience and the actual sights at hand. In most cases this is an adequate solution, but in rare cases we might need to choose the very best location based on all that we know about the three LOPs. These can be celestial sights, or they could be three compass or gyro bearing lines. More to the point, they could be two bearings of standard accuracy and a range line (transit) that can be a very accurate LOP, or equivalently, one very good celestial sight and two that were not as good due to poor horizon or fewer sights in the sequence.

In short, if we are to apply more sophisticated analysis, we need to have enough extra data to justify it, which can be expressed as the individual uncertainties in each sight, called their variances.

It can be shown that if these variances are all the same (no one sight better than another), and there is no systematic error that applies to all of them, then the most likely position is located at what is called the symmedian point of the triangle, which is discussed at length at online math resources. It is frankly fairly tedious to graphically plot this point, but worth noting that it is *not* any of the common centroids we might have considered. This does not distract from the practical solution we usually use underway, because we are fine-tuning the analysis here, and assuming knowledge we do not always have.

Once you are convinced that the variances are not the same, then the symmedian point is no longer correct. For example, if one line (of a terrestrial fix) is a range, then that should bias the fix toward that line, and the other two compass bearings are effectively just showing where you are on that line.

We have developed a solution to the most likely position that is relatively easy to evaluate by hand, and very easy to solve with a calculator or programmed function.

The result for the most likely position P can be written as:

$$P = q_1 Q_1 + q_2 Q_2 + q_3 Q_3,$$

where $q_i = s_i^2 \sigma_i^2 / \Sigma (s_j^2 \sigma_j^2)$.

In this formalism the most likely point is determined from the sides of the triangle (s_i) and the variance of each line (σ_i) without reference to the intersection angles.

Consider a sample triangle of sides 10, 9, and 13 that have corresponding variances of 1, 2, and 3. The units are arbitrary, chosen for convenience of measurement on the nautical chart or plotting sheet in use. Once the LOPs have been plotted, it is the task of the navigator to assign the corresponding variances.

For a graphic solution, it is easiest to use rectilinear co-ordinates (x.y), as shown in Figure A5-1. The orientation of the coordinates is chosen to align with one of the LOPs, and the location of the third point is measured from the chart in the same units, (5.7, 6.9) in this case. In this example:

$\Sigma (s_j^2 \sigma_j^2) = 100 \times 1 + 81 \times 4 + 169 \times 9 = 1945$, and

$$q_1 = 100/1945 = 0.051,$$

$$q_2 = 324/1945 = 0.167,$$

$$q_3 = 1521/1945 = 0.782.$$

Then with $Q_1 = (0, 0)$, $Q_2 = (13, 0)$, and $Q_3 = (5.7, 6.9)$, we get:

$$P = 0.051 \times (0,0) + 0.167 \times (13,0) + 0.782 \times (5.7,6.9)$$

$$= (0, 0) + (2.2, 0) + (4.5, 5.4)$$

$$= (6.7, 5.4).$$

This process may seem complex at first glance, but that is tied in large part to the compact notation. After working a few examples the procedure becomes more fluid. This is the first solution we have seen that offers a fast practical way to answer this question accounting for variances in the LOPs.

———

* Adapted from *Celestial Navigation: A Complete Home Study Course, Second Edition* By David Burch (Starpath Publications, 2017). Original work by Richard Rice and David Burch, 2012, unpublished.)

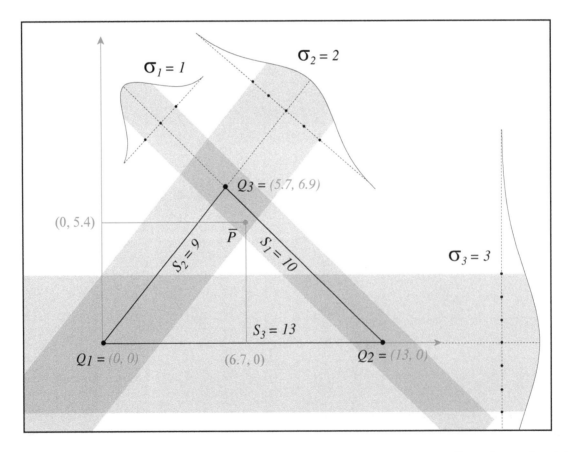

Figure A5-1 *Most likely point P (6.7, 5.4) determined from three LOPs, without systematic error. The variance of each LOP is shown schematically to match the units chosen to measure the sides of the triangle from the chart. If the units were miles, a centroid choice would be wrong by 3 miles.*

Appendix 6. References

Books

1. *U.S. Chart No. 1: Symbols, Abbreviations, and Terms used on Paper and Electronic Navigational Charts*, NOAA and NGA, 2013

2. *Integrated Bridge Systems Vol 1: ECDIS and Positioning* By Andy Norris (The Nautical Institute, 2010)

3. *Admiralty Guide to the Practical Use of ENCs, 2nd ed. NP 231* (UKHO, 2016)

4. Bowditch: *American Practical Navigator, NGA Pub 9* by Nathaniel Bowditch

5. *Radar for Mariners, Revised Edition* By David Burch (McGraw-Hill, 2013)

6. *Modern Marine Weather, Second Edition* By David Burch (Starpath Publications, 2016)

7. *Inland and Coastal Navigation, Second Edition* By David Burch (Starpath Publications, 2013)

Internet Links [Support for this book, including link updates as needed, at **www.starpath.com/ENC**]

1. U.S. Chart No. 1:
https://www.nauticalcharts.noaa.gov/mcd/chartno1.htm

2. IHO ENC and ECDIS Standards in Force:
www.iho.int/mtg_docs/enc/ECDIS-ENC_StdsIn_Force.htm

3. IHO Catalog of International ENC:
https://www.iho.int/srv1/index.php?option=com_content&view=article&id=393&Itemid=424&lang=en

4. Starpath eNav Trainer—GPS and AIS Simulator:
https://www.starpath.com/enav

5. NOAA nautical chart inquires:
https://www.nauticalcharts.noaa.gov/nsd/services.htm

6. UKHO H-Notes app for chart and pub discrepancies:
https://www.admiralty.co.uk/maritime-safety-information/hydrographic-notes

7. Wikipedia on AIS:
https://en.wikipedia.org/wiki/Automatic_identification_system

8. AIS at USCG Navigation Center (navcen):
https://www.navcen.uscg.gov/?pageName=AISmain

9. S-57 Objects and Attributes Online Catalog:
http://www.caris.com/s-57

10. NMEA Revealed:
http://catb.org/gpsd/NMEA.html

11. IMO Documents:
http://www.navcen.uscg.gov/?pageName=mscResolutions

12. S-57 Appendix A, IHO Object catalog:
https://www.iho.int/iho_pubs/standard/S-57Ed3.1/31ApAch1.pdf

13. History of electronic charting:
http://www.starpath.com/ENC

14. Air gap system for live air draft:
https://tidesandcurrents.noaa.gov/press/oaklandbaybridge.html

15. Value of NOAA PORTS services:
https://tidesandcurrents.noaa.gov/publications/Value_of_PORTS_to_the_Nation_Aug_2014.pdf

16. Accuracy of NOAA chart data:
https://noaacoastsurvey.wordpress.com/2016/04/08/how-accurate-are-nautical-charts/

17. Interactive Navigation Rules Handbook:
www.starpath.com/navrules/NavigationRulesHandbook.html

18. World Magnetic Model and geomag software:
https://www.ngdc.noaa.gov/geomag/models.shtml

19. NZ ENC Guidelines:
http://www.linz.govt.nz/docs/hydro/stds-and-specs/encspecv1-3.pdf

20. U.S. Coast Pilot:
https://www.nauticalcharts.noaa.gov/nsd/cpdownload.htm

21. Bowditch, American Practical Navigator, NGA Pub. 9:
http://msi.nga.mil/NGAPortal/MSI.portal?_nfpb=true&_pageLabel=msi_portal_page_62&pubCode=0002

23. S-66 Facts about ENC:
https://www.iho.int/iho_pubs/standard/S-66/S-66_e1.0.0_EN.pdf

24. High Resolution Rapid Refresh (HRRR) model:
https://rapidrefresh.noaa.gov/hrrr

25. Grib files for meteorology and oceanography:
http://www.saildocs.com

26. Download NOAA Charts and access Online ENC Viewer:
https://www.nauticalcharts.noaa.gov

27. MACHC online ENC viewer:
http://www.iho-machc.org

Index

CPSIA information can be obtained
at www.ICGtesting.com
Printed in the USA
BVHW02s0829150918
527591BV00012B/89/P